Religion and the Domestication of Dissent

Religion in Culture: Studies in Social Contest and Construction

Series Editor: Russell T. McCutcheon, University of Alabama

This series is based on the assumption that those practices we commonly call religious are social practices that are inextricably embedded in various contingent, cultural worlds. Authors in this series therefore do not see the practices of religion occupying a socially or politically autonomous zone, as is the case for those who use 'and' as the connector between "religion" and "culture." Rather, the range of human performances that the category "religion" identifies can be demystified by translating them into fundamentally social terms; they should therefore be seen as ways of waging the ongoing contest between groups vying for influence and dominance in intra- and inter-cultural arenas. Although not limited to one historical period, cultural site, or methodological approach, each volume exemplifies the tactical contribution to be made to the human sciences by writers who refuse to study religion as irreducibly religious; instead, each author conceptualizes religion— as well as the history of scholarship on religion—as among the various *arts de faire*, or practices of everyday life, upon which human communities routinely draw when defining and reproducing themselves in opposition to others.

Forthcoming titles in the series:

The Symbolic Jesus: Historical Scholarship, Judaism and the Construction of Contemporary Identity
William Arnal

It's Just Another Story: The Politics of Remembering the Earliest Christian
Willi Braun

Religion and the Domestication of Dissent
or
How to Live in a Less than Perfect Nation

Russell T. McCutcheon

LONDON   OAKVILLE

Published by

Equinox Publishing Ltd

UK: Unit 6, The Village, 101 Amies St., London SW11 2JW

US: 28 Main Street, Oakville, CT 06779

www.equinoxpub.com

First published 2005 by Equinox Publishing Ltd.

© Russell T. McCutcheon 2005

British Library Cataloguing-in-Publication Data

A catalogue record for this book is available from the British Library.

ISBN   1-84553-000-4   (hardback)
        1-84553-001-2   (paperback)

Library of Congress Cataloging-in-Publication Data

McCutcheon, Russell T., 1961-
  Religion and the domestication of dissent, or, How to live in a less than perfect nation / Russell T. McCutcheon.-- 1st ed.
      p. cm. -- (Religion in culture)
  Includes bibliographical references and index.
  ISBN 1-84553-000-4 -- ISBN 1-84553-001-2 (pbk.)
  1. Religion and politics. 2. Religion--Philosophy. I. Title:
Religion and the domestication of dissent. II. Title: How to live in a
less than perfect nation. III. Title. IV. Series.
  BL65.P7M355 2005
  200'.72--dc22
                            2004013026

Typeset by ISB Typesetting, Sheffield, UK
iain@sheffieldtypesetting.com

Printed and bound in Great Britain by Antony Rowe Ltd, Chippenham, Wiltshire

Contents

Preface

Consider three recent episodes, all of which took place in February 2004.

Returning to Chicago's O'Hare International Airport to fly back to Birmingham, Alabama, after visiting the University of Chicago for the weekend, I was picked up by a cab driver who was originally from Tanzania. Although the traffic was not that bad, it was still a forty-minute ride, so our conversation moved from talk of the weather, our shared nostalgia for our separate homelands, and the Democratic presidential primaries which were then taking place, eventually getting around to Janet Jackson's breast-baring at the 2004 Superbowl's half-time show. Upon learning that I studied comparative religions, she told me that she was Muslim and commented on the unfortunate impact of Christian missionaries at home. Sooner or later, the conversation worked around to what it was like living as a Muslim in the U.S. after September 11, 2001. Lamenting the current state of affairs, she sighed and shook her head, saying, "radicals have hijacked Islam."

Later that same day, while awaiting my flight, an announcement came over the airport loudspeaker. "Roman Catholic Mass will be celebrated in the airport chapel at 4:00 p.m. Everyone is welcome to attend."

A few days later, a reporter for my university's online student newspaper, *Dateline Alabama* (http://www.datelinealabama.com) came to my office to discuss Mel Gibson's much publicized film, *The Passion of the Christ* (2004). Why, she wanted to ask a Religious Studies professor, had so much attention been given to historical detail in the film—such as having actors speak Aramaic and Latin—but the character Jesus was still Caucasian, presumably looking nothing like an average male inhabitant of the Mediterranean region some two thousand years ago. "Doesn't this insult other people, such as African-Americans?" she asked. "Isn't Mel Gibson's Jesus too white?"

What these three episodes all have in common is not simply that I was there for each, or that they all took place in the same month. What strikes me as rather more significant is that each is an example of how historically embedded social actors steer the course through their semantically ambiguous worlds, building identities and coalitions of identities, by resorting to what I'll simply refer to as the rhetoric of authenticity. But, despite what those who employ these rhetorics might think—everyone from an expatriate cab driver in Chicago making claims about what constitutes authentic Islam, to a Hollywood director selling the meaning of the Gospel to viewing audiences worldwide—their claims to authenticity all take place in ever-changing historical circumstances, ensuring that these discourses must operate on a sliding scale where some things are a little more authentic than others, and some are authentic but only some of the time.

Because a white Jesus who speaks Aramaic is both familiar and strange, it is evident that authenticity is a slippery boundary marker, always in motion relative to a community's changing interests and contexts. But since members of the group take their own identity to be enduring and uniform—despite significant gaps within the group—their assertions of authenticity efficiently gloss over an unresolvable dilemma, i.e., how to have permanence, identity, and meaning in the midst of historical happenstance. Such rhetorics do this by creating the *impression* of two interrelated states of affairs: limitless inclusion and sharp distinction: apparently, "all are welcome" to a ritual that just happens to function to set one group apart from another (whether that be those outside the Church or those within it who have yet to partake of their First Communion). Although everyone is welcome, I imagine that not everyone can have a wafer. Or, despite reports of Pope John Paul II lending his imprimatur to Gibson's film—"It is as it was," Vatican insiders were reported to have said the Pope concluded after a private screening of the film before its release, though Cardinal Stanislaw Dziwisw, the Pope's private secretary, subsequently denied that the Pope had said any such thing—evangelical Protestants, many of whom would vehemently argue that Catholics are not even Christians (much less saved), have been flocking to theaters and buying up blocks of seats to this traditionalist Catholic depiction of Jesus' last twelve hours. Apparently, a brief, ecumenical unity is possible when otherwise competing groups huddle in the dark around what they each take to be a representation of their ahistorical, originary source. Much like the movie screen itself, this speculative origin is a blank slate onto which they can each project their individual (and, perhaps, mutually exclusive) self-images. Yet things are not quite so simple, or civil, when they all leave the cool of the theater and their interests clash in the light of day.

These rhetorics of uniform origins and timeless principles, of pure intentions versus degraded expressions, and of pristine insides versus ambiguous outsides—all of which we find everywhere from Chicago cabs to darkened theaters and scholarly monographs—are eminently useful to virtually any group engaging in the necessary sleight of hand we call social formation. But their utility is limited, of course, because conflicting groups are often more alike than their members can afford to recognize; and because coalitions have internal contests that must go unseen if their cooperative work is to continue, sooner or later the cracks show through. It is in this way that rhetorics undermine themselves and make evident difference where similarity was once cherished, and similarity where difference once caught our attention. Just as with the three little girls' infectious nursery rhyme that I heard just today at lunch—"Girls go to college to get more knowledge; boys go to Jupiter to get more stupider"—upon closer examination, the relationships that we hold dear, those that assist us to understand ourselves in relation and opposition to others, provide the undoing of our cherished similarities and differences. For, despite their whimsical efforts to distinguish themselves from "stupider" little boys, thereby simultaneously marking their commonly shared (and, I presume they thought, superior) status, these little girls' ungrammatical chant put them in the same boat as their untutored male counterparts.

And it is just this sort of rhetorical hocus-pocus that is the focus of the following short volume.

Tuscaloosa, Alabama
March 2004

Acknowledgements

In producing this brief book, I am indebted to a number of people—friends, colleagues, and students—for their influence on my thinking. Some of them read portions of the following chapters or, knowing what I was up to, made important suggestions regarding material that I ought to consider including or shared with me some of their own unpublished work on related topics. Foremost among friends and colleagues who deserve mention are: Bill Arnal, Herb Berg, Willi Braun, Julie Ingersoll, Greg Johnson, Darlene Juschka, Bruce Lincoln, Jack Llewellyn, Tomoko Masuzawa, Tim Murphy, Kurtis Schaeffer, and Jonathan Z. Smith, to whom this book is dedicated. Also, some of the students I have had the privilege to teach—in Knoxville, Tennessee, Springfield, Missouri, and now Tuscaloosa, Alabama—who, perhaps unknowingly, have made important contributions to helping me think through this project, deserve mention here as well. Among them are: Clay Arnold, Guy Cutting, Kim Davis (who kindly assisted in the final stages of this book's production), Scott Elliott, Pedja Klasnja, Jason Miller, John Parrish, Mark Premo-Hopkins, Josalyn Randall, Leslie Smith, Kyle Stephens, and Matt Waggoner. My thanks also goes to Betty Dickey, our Department's Senior Office Administrator, who helps to tame the unruliness of day-to-day life in a university, often (and lucky for me!) before it reaches my desk. I would also like to acknowledge Bryan Rennie and Phil Tite for inviting a far shorter version of what became the following, to be included in their co-edited book *Underlying Terror: Religious Studies Perspectives on the War on Terrorism* (State University of New York Press, 2005); without that kind invitation I more than likely would not have kept writing to produce much of the following.

I would also like to thank Janet Joyce, founder of Equinox Publishers, for her continued interest in supporting my work, as well as express my debt to her staff, especially Sarah Norman, the freelance copyeditor who did such a fine job on this text.

These acknowledgements would be incomplete without mention of the woman who has been my wife since 1985, Marcia Hay-McCutcheon, who, in 2004, completed her own PhD at the University of Iowa. My pride for her accomplishments these past four years is surpassed only by my love for her.

An earlier version of chapter 1 was presented as part of an April 2004 conference on "Conflicts at the Border of Religions and the Secular" sponsored by the Center for the Study of Religion and Conflict at Arizona State University. I would therefore like to express my debt to Linell Cady for the invitation to visit Tempe, Arizona, to participate in the work of her newly established Center. This paper was also presented at the University of Regina and the University of Alberta, in Edmonton, Canada, both in September 2004. I am indebted to Bill Arnal and Willi Braun, respectively, for arranging this trip and for being my generous hosts. This chapter was also presented in February 2005 at Syracuse University's Department of Religion, as their Spring Symposium lecture; my thanks to Patricia Cox Miller, for extending their kind invitation, and to their graduate students for suggesting my name as the speaker.

Earlier versions of chapter 2—which is based on a far longer review essay written for the Canadian journal, *Studies in Religion* and published in 2004—were presented at Wilfrid Laurier University and the University of Chicago, both in February 2004, as part of workshops devoted to the place of personal religious commitment in the classroom. I would not only like to thank Faydra Shapiro and Lucy Pick for organizing each of these two events and for including me among those invited to speak, but I would also like to express my debt to Michel Desjardins (the first person for whom I ever worked as a teaching assistant while at the University of Toronto in the early 1990s, who is currently the Department Chair at Wilfrid Laurier), as well as to Bruce Lincoln and Jonathan Z. Smith, all of whom played the role of gracious hosts, providing wonderful meals and even better conversation while I was a guest in Waterloo and Chicago, respectively.

Small portions of some of the following chapters were published as "The Perils of Having One's Cake and Eating it Too," a paper published in *Religious Studies Review* (2004) as a response to a November 2003 panel on comparative religion textbooks, which was part of the annual meeting of the American Academy of Religion in Atlanta, Georgia. Material on the ossuary of James derives from my "Filling in the Cracks with Resin: A Reply to John Burris's, 'Text and Context in the Study of Religion'," *Method & Theory in the Study of Religion* 15/3 (2004): 284–303; and small portions of other material was originally presented as part of my March 2003 Delton L. Scudder Memorial Lecture in the Department of Religion at the University of Florida (subsequently published in *Method & Theory in the Study of Religion* 2004). My thanks to Gene Thursby for extending the kind invitation to visit Gainesville, Florida, to deliver this annual lecture.

The Afterword's quotation of material from "South Park" is quoted with permission.

...and they must have learned how to keep silent in order to remain your friend.

Friedrich Nietzsche (1986, 148)

For Jonathan,
who taught me to look for the choices people make,
and to see whether they are willing to bear the costs.

1 "Religion" and the Lust for Dogmatic Rule

For some time there has been a growing number of scholars who have begun to see the classification "religion," and its relation to the equally interesting category "secular," to have a practical effect on the ways in which people in Europe and North America—as well as those who have been impacted by their exported economic and political systems—think and act. Perhaps this is best, and most recently, phrased by the anthropologist Talal Asad, in his book, *Formations of the Secular*: "What interests me particularly," he writes,

> is the attempt to construct categories of the secular and the religious in terms of which modern living is required to take place, and nonmodern peoples are invited to assess their adequacy. (2003, 14)

If, as anthropologists long ago concluded, the distinction between soil and dirt refers *not* to some essential feature in the objects being classified but, instead, is an effect of the interests of the group of classifiers who employ the distinction as a means of establishing and charting a particular social world comprised of a system of dos and don'ts, then the group of scholars to which I refer are interested in the social effects of those common distinctions that go by such names as religion/politics, sacred/secular, or faith/practice. These classifications are understood to be used by groups of people *not* because of their uncanny ability to name some deep or critically important feature in the objects or actions so named (regardless what the users of these categories think they intend by their use), but, as with soil/dirt, clean/ unclean, text/context, citizen/foreigner, and insider/outsider, because of the ways in which these classifications, once entrenched in people's minds, actions, and social institutions, then enable groups to differentiate themselves both within the limits of their own group (i.e., to rank the many degrees of group memberships) and in distinction from others. In the process, they are thereby enabled to allot or withhold resources and status accordingly.

This shift in scholarly focus—from writing a history of a religion or tackling a study of politics *and* religion to writing a history of "religion" and tackling a study of the politics *of* "religion"—may, at first, sound counter-intuitive to some readers. Such readers are therefore invited to consider reading two previous works of mine, chapter 10 of *Critics Not Caretakers* (2001), "Our 'Special' Promise: Scholars of Religion and the Politics of Tolerance," and chapter 12 of *The Discipline of Religion* (2003), "Religion and the Governable Self"; the arguments of these two chapters could be seen as the set-up for the punch-line of the following. Read together, they take as their point of departure what has by now become a truism of the modern world, and which—precisely *because* it is understood as a truism—is therefore ripe for rethinking: that those aspects of our social worlds that we come to know as (i.e., classify as) religion are, by strictest definition, essentially concerned with trans-human and thus apolitical deep belief and morality—both of which are encoded seamlessly within such things as the meaning of a text, the purpose of a rite, or essence of a symbol—that, when nurtured, are thought to bring about tolerance in a pluralistic state. Based on this widely accepted folk knowledge, we become perplexed when so-called religious people do what many of us take to be bad things, as in when those people we term fundamentalists commandeer, let's say for the sake of argument, jet airliners and fly them into buildings. Or when anti-abortion protestors kill doctors. Or when someone proclaims that God commands them to marry more than one spouse. For those who presume that the practices we group together and name religion are self-evidently set apart from the messy world of politics and economics, a form of cognitive dissonance sets in when confronted with such seemingly counter-intuitive actions and claims.

Anyone who watched the North American television coverage after the attacks of September 11, 2001, will know that making sense of such behaviors poses a considerable interpretive challenge for such people; lucky for them, countless learned commentators are up to the challenge, authoritatively wielding such troublesome notions as "cult" and "fanatic" on the evening news, endeavoring to tell us precisely how it is radically different from the common-sense worlds we all inhabit, how such deviance could have happened, and what we can do about it. Of course we don't entertain that social life is comprised of a series of competing interests around which sub-groups organize to compete for limited resources (everything from prestige to oil), and that such "deviant" groups are merely putting their brand of oppositional politics into practice much as we routinely put our brand of dominant politics into practice. We also do not entertain that our own government's foreign and domestic policies might be understood— correctly or not, in our opinion—by others as a form of violent behavior that, like it or not, some people think needs to be met with retaliatory violence. No, this we can never entertain for, as Noam Chomsky has suc- cinctly phrased it, "that would require at the very least a willingness on the part of the educated classes to look into the mirror instead of restricting themselves to lamentations on the crimes of official enemies" (2003, 53). As the evil Queen in "Snow White" found out, sometimes mirrors are dangerous things to look into, for they are apt to tell you things you might not want to hear; it's likely to be safer to offer up grandiose theories of social deviance and religious fanaticism, since they enable us to dismiss other people's behaviors before ever really considering just what we're all competing over.

As an example, take scholars who are perplexed by the manner in which distant (in temporal as well as cultural space) populations either remain inactive or willingly participate in actions that we term genocides. Such (in)activity then becomes the object of scholarly fascination: how could they stand by and do nothing? Or, how could they willingly participate? Anticipating the eventual trial of Saddam Hussein, commentators are already beginning to ask how the Iraqi people were able either to remain idle or carry out the admittedly atrocious activities of Hussein's government.[1] Although not wishing to appear to minimize the horrendous nature of some (or should I say many?) governments' (mis)deeds against members of their own populations and those of other nations, I admit that I am rather perplexed as to why the curiosity of such scholars is limited to "some governments." For instance, we are never curious as to why we as a social group devote considerable intellectual energy, labor, and dramatic amounts of capital developing and marketing such things as laundry soaps capable of making our already white whites even whiter, "longer-lasting" air fresheners, and erectile disfunction medications for the aging baby boomer generation, while something as easily addressed as childhood diarrhea continues to kill tremendous numbers of children all across the Third World.[2] To stick with this one simple example, given that the worldwide incidence of childhood diarrhea is linked to issues of basic sanitation, it is estimated by the Christian Children's Fund that "drinking-water and sanitation improvements could reduce the overall incidence of infant and child diarrhea by $\frac{1}{4}$ and cut total infant and child mortality by more than $\frac{1}{2}$."[3] Yet consumers and executives who devote their energies to deciding whether Coke or Pepsi are more refreshing lose no sleep whatsoever over participating in a socio-economic system that functions to horde wealth. Perhaps it is this wealth—along with both the ironic distance from our own actions that it purchases for us, as well as the difficulty many people have with developing a critique of structure-wide *systems* as opposed to the ease with which they vent their disapproval of bad *individuals*—that allows us to be perplexed by the actions (or inactions) of others, those whom we are able to hold to an infinitely higher standard than the one by which we measure the motivations and impact of our own (mis)deeds.[4]

The very fact that the actions of others pose such an interpretive challenge for us, prompting us to trot out a host of troublesome concepts and stereotypes, should make us curious, and should draw our attention to the set of assumptions "in terms of which," to quote from Asad once again, "modern living [i.e., contests over modern meaning-making and social formation] is required to take place." That our television network's talking heads and our newspaper editorial writers never seem to fret over how to understand the apparent contradiction between our unbridled celebration of our own egalitarian ideals, on the one hand, and our consistent efforts to export our political and economic system to distant lands at the point of a gun barrel, on the other, suggests just how deeply implicated both our pundits and their sense of what constitutes a problem are in but one way of acting in the world. For when "we" sponsor violence (let's say, financially supporting Iraq during its almost decade-long war with Iran, a time period in which many of the Iraqi atrocities took place that somehow bother us so greatly now, twenty years later)[5] and when "our" sons and daughters are prepared to die helping to reproduce a particular way of life it is apparently always for a good reason—the promotion and realization of our group's material interests is always a good reason, we tell ourselves. Yet when "they" sponsor violence in pursuit of competing material interests and when "their" sons and daughters are prepared to die protecting a different way of life (and, given assumptions concerning gender that circulate widely in our own group, it is particularly troubling to many when young women are prepared to die for a cause), it is apparently always for the wrong reason. It is within this unwieldy interpretive, political fray—a space in which competing sets of social interests meet—that I propose we consider the use of the category "religion" and the attendant presumption that a uniform aspect *within* the world (call it faith, or experience, or spirituality, or meaning, or human nature, etc.) somehow escapes the usually operating constraints and ambiguities *of* the world.

Most recently, I think of three examples of the now considerable body of problem-solving literature that explores the religious causes of violence: Charles Kimball's *When Religion Becomes Evil* (2002); Jessica Stein's *Terror in the Name of God: Why Religious Militants Kill* (2003); and Mark Jurgensmeyer's far more academically rigorous *Terror in the Mind of God: The Global Rise of Religious Violence* (2001). Although they are not all equally sensationalistic, all three books use "religion" in their efforts to explain good people gone bad, i.e., religious people engaging in overt political opposition. But what if the very distinction between religion and politics, as with that between good and evil, belief and behavior, insider and outsider, is itself what ought to attract our attention? What if we took seriously that no one, not even scholars, can escape history and, thus, sidestep the need to position oneself within a busy economy of competing claims and interests? Then we might realize that all we have is a mass of historical agents—including such writers as Kimball, Stein, and Jurgensmeyer!—contesting shared identities and access to scarce resources by means of their competing classification systems and the various types of force used to implement them. Furthermore, we might come to see that the very tools we employ in our academic attempts to understand why so-called fanatics do what they do are themselves among the ways in which our own group works to gain its competitive edge in a busy social economy. In fact, just labeling oppositional groups as "fanatics" and "extremists" has already won half the battle, for there is no longer any need to take their motivations seriously—whether or not one agrees with them. Commentators, whether popular or academic, who make use of such distinctions of good/evil and spiritual/fanatical, then, might be understood as but one more site of this ongoing contest, rather than as disinterested observers of the political process.[6]

Of course, there is a well-established scholarly tradition upon which such commentators are drawing; although it is tempting to call it an intellectual tradition, in keeping with the tactical goals of this book, I'd prefer not to lodge our object of study within the confines of the disembodied intellect. Instead, I choose to refer to it as a loosely related network of political actors distinguished by a common rhetorical strategy that they employ to achieve a variety of ends. That strategy is nicely represented in the US by the still celebrated nineteenth-century psychologist of religion, William James (1842–1910). Although the privatization, or sentimentalization, of what might otherwise be understood as ambiguous and thus contestable public performance goes back much further than James's writings on religion (e.g., the Protestant Reformation's rhetoric of sincere, inner faith over insincere, external works is among the most effective use of this rhetoric on a large scale), in the context of recent US history James is perhaps the best example of this technique, if for no other reason than the continued utility of his work for those who cite it to authorize their own concerning just what gets to count as authentically human.

Near the opening of a chapter entitled, "The Value of Saintliness," in his famous Gifford Lectures of 1901–1902 (soon after published as *The Varieties of Religious Experience* [1902][7]), James writes as follows:

> The word "religion," as ordinarily used, is equivocal. A survey of history shows us that, as a rule, religious geniuses attack disciples, and produce groups of sympathizers. When these groups get strong enough to "organize" themselves, they become ecclesiastical institutions with corporate ambitions of their own. The spirit of politics and the lust of dogmatic rule are then apt to enter and to contaminate the originally innocent thing; so that when we hear the word "religion" nowadays, we think inevitably of some "church" or other; and to some persons the word "church" suggests so much hypocrisy and tyranny and meanness and tenacity of superstition that in a wholesale undiscerning way they glory in saying that they are "down" on religion altogether. Even we who belong to churches do not exempt other churches than our own from the general condemnation.
>
> But in this course of lectures ecclesiastical institutions hardly concern us at all. The religious experience which we are studying is that which lives itself out within the private breast. (1985, 334–35)

There may be no more succinct statement of the position whose political effects are examined in the following essays. Before proceeding, it might be useful to see that behind James's famous definition of religion—"the feelings, acts, and experiences of individual men in their solitude, so far as they apprehend themselves to stand in relation to whatever they may consider the divine" (1985, 31)—there are the following three presumptions:

- An inner, pure, and dynamic experience is both logically and chronologically prior to historically-embedded human behavior (i.e., "the originally innocent thing").
- This experience is best exemplified in individuals who, by means of their charisma, are the driving force of a social group's development and growth (i.e., "religious geniuses").
- Once organized, the public behavior of the genius's associates, insomuch as it is but an expression of the prior, inner sentiment, is prone to deterioration and, lamentably, apt to be bogged down in such things as doctrine, ritual, and institution (i.e., weighted down by "the lust for dogmatic rule").

With these presumptions in mind, James understandably says from the outset that his study is devoted *not* to the "ordinary religious believer, who follows the conventional observances of his country … [for] his religion has been made for him by others, communicated to him by tradition, determined to fixed forms by imitation, and retained by habit." Given his presumption that the driving force in history is the lone, charismatic genius, it makes sense that James concludes that "[i]t would profit us little to study this second-hand religious life" (1985, 6). Instead of studying religion "as a dull habit," James seeks to study the "acute fever" of the religious genius who possesses "the original experiences which were the pattern-setters to all this mass of suggested feeling and imitated conduct" (1985, 6).

With such oppositions as those between original and imitation, inner and outer, experience and behavior, all up and running, James reasonably concludes that the category "religion" is an equivocal term, signifying for his readers *both* the "contagious … spontaneous religious spirit" (1985, 337) that lives in the human heart—hence his (and many other people's) preference for the category "religious experience"—as well as its sadly degraded outer manifestations. These organized expressions bear the name of "church," which signifies a sadly repressive social institution that, by definition, acts as a force to "stop all later bubblings of the fountain from which in purer days it drew its own supply of inspiration" [1985, 337]). Or, to update James's thesis, we might reply in the words of contemporary popular culture by saying, "I'm not religious, but I *am* spiritual."

Although my hope is that the following persuades readers that this rhetoric of insides and outsides, origins and degradations, spirituality and institutions, is alive and well in the twenty-first century, for the moment consider how, precisely one hundred years after James delivered these words in Edinburgh, another Gifford lecturer, this time the noted philosopher and ethicist Charles Taylor, drew on the same distinctions. In a series of lectures delivered in Vienna a couple of years after his own 1999 Gifford Lectures, Taylor—the well-known author of such works as *Sources of the Self: The Making of the Modern Identity* (1989) and *The Ethics of Authenticity* (1991)—

celebrated James's influence while also attempting to update his thesis, to take into account that the social *expression* of religious experience may itself be but one more variety, or one more form, as Taylor puts it, of religion that James, in his exclusive emphasis on private experience, unfortunately disregarded. Acknowledging that James "has trouble getting beyond a certain individualism" (2002, 23), which prevents him from understanding "the phenomenon of collective religious life" (p. 24), Taylor proposes that updating James means considering how "the link between the believer and the divine (or whatever), may be essentially *mediated* by corporate, ecclesial life" (p. 23; emphasis added).

To update James's work, Taylor argues that "some propositional formulations are unavoidable" to articulate precisely what the "sacramental way of life ... is all about" (2002, 26), even going so far as to entertain, along with Ludwig Wittgenstein, "that the very idea of an experience that is in no way formulated is impossible" (p. 26; citing *Philosophical Investigations* I, 261[8]). Since "[a]ll experiences require some vocabulary ... [that] are inevitably in large part handed to us in the first place by our society" (pp. 27–28)— whether that social vocabulary entails "ordinary unavoidable description," on the one hand, or is "authoritatively theorized by some official magisterium that can lean on you for the heterodoxy of your experience" (p. 27)—Taylor concludes that James's study must be revised somewhat, so that it can take into account the fact that "[t]here are (what are in one sense) individual experiences that are immensely *enhanced* by the sense that they are shared" (p. 28; emphasis added).

At this point we must pause to recognize that the social dimension Taylor introduces seems to be a considerable gain for those of us who wish to take seriously that human beings are unavoidably social creatures and are not, as James seems to have assumed, lamentably stuck with inhabiting a social world. After all, as Taylor acknowledges near the close of his first lecture, "[t]he ideas, the understanding with which we live our lives, *shape* directly what we could call religious experience; and these languages, these vocabularies, are never those simply of the individual" (2002, 28; emphasis added). But what sort of gain is this? To answer this question I draw specific attention to the italicized words in the above quotations: experience is *enhanced* and *shaped*. Although I wish not to place too much emphasis on the choice of these words, it strikes me as profoundly significant that Taylor is *not* arguing that one's social location *determines* one's experience, *causes* one's experience, or *makes* one's experience. Instead, much as with James himself, Taylor presupposes some sort of inner experience that is expressed to varying degrees of satisfaction; of course Taylor does not lament the limitations of this expression to the degree that James did; but, nonetheless, they agree on the priority of the inner world over the outer, insomuch as the outer shapes the dynamism of the inner. This is none other than the common technique of determining the deep meaning of a text or a behavior by reading it into its varied contexts; while this seems to be a significant gain for the socially inclined scholar (much as Clifford Geertz's contributions toward "thick interpretation" in anthropology were once seen as a significant advance over prior generation's shallow descriptivist work), the many contexts in which some action is performed or some text is read are merely presumed to comprise the contingent medium that houses the manifested expression of a prior thing we call meaning or intention that is thought somehow to reside within the behavior or the text. So, despite Taylor's promise to update and advance James's individualistic tendency, we see that the more things change, the more they remain the same.

To support this point further, consider the example that Taylor uses to drive home his argument:

> I am sitting at home watching the local hockey team win the Stanley Cup. I rejoice in this. But the sense of my joy here is *framed* by my understanding that thousands of fans all over the city, some gathered at rinkside, others also in their living rooms, are sharing this moment of exultation.

With this example in mind, he concludes:

> There are certain emotions you can have in solidarity that you can't have alone; the experience mutates into something else by the fact that it is shared. How much of what James thinks of as individual experience is socially *enhanced* or *affected* in this way? (2002, 28–29; emphasis added)

As a displaced Canadian who grew up a dyed-in-the-wool Toronto Maple Leafs hockey fan (whose sworn enemies, by the way, were the fans of the Montreal Canadiens, the "local hockey team" to which Taylor—an emeritus professor of philosophy and political science at McGill University in Montreal—no doubt refers), I too have had my share of solitary experiences of joy—and, if you knew the Leafs' win/loss record since they last won the Stanley Cup in 1967, solitary experiences of disappointment while seated in front of the TV on a Saturday night (which is, for those who have ears to hear, affectionately known as "Hockey Night in Canada"). However, having lived and worked in the US south for over a decade, I would no longer call myself a hockey fan since games are rarely broadcast and, when they are, the play-by-play announcers describe the game to their US audience in such a way that a fan versed in the game feels like an untutored moron. For example, one national US television network once experimented with a computer-enhanced graphic that provided the televised image of the hockey puck with a colorful aura as it zipped around the rink, supposedly making it easier for fans to follow. As one weaned on televised hockey games instead of baseball games or golf matches, and hence not all that accustomed to watching a tiny white ball soar against a faint blue sky, I could never figure out why television executives thought that a black puck moving across white ice was all that difficult for US viewers to see.[9] Come to think of it, placing a glowing graphic around a baseball would, more than likely, be seen by many as a desecration of *the American past-time*. That I therefore found it patronizing that the network would fiddle with my experience of the game makes it all too obvious that the social location of my beginnings, north of the 49th parallel, has indeed *shaped* my experience.

But as I first read Taylor's example—perhaps because I read it while preparing to teach his book to a group of undergraduate students in Tuscaloosa, Alabama, where frost and ice, let alone snow, are seldom seen and where you must order "hot tea" to get what I once thought was simply called "tea"—it dawned on me just how wide of the mark Taylor was in using this example to make his point. For what he presents as the inner emotions that prompt him to rejoice (e.g., his feelings of joy and exultation), and which, he suggests, can be enhanced in a social setting (e.g., watching the big game with friends at a local bar), are hardly pre-social, inner dispositions that are merely *shaped*, *mediated*, and *framed* by the location of their expression. For my students, for whom "arena" signifies somewhere that you play basketball, not hockey, could hardly identify with an argument that took for granted that exultation attends watching your team win what some people simply refer to as "the Cup." I would therefore argue that the experience of the game is itself the product of—and is not simply shaped or framed by—differing social locations. To stick with Taylor's imagery, the frame does not enhance the picture; instead, in focusing attention by enacting exclusion, the frame *transforms* mere background into a picture! To phrase it in terms of text and context, it is not simply that the context is the site in which the text's prior meaning is *expressed* but, instead, the text and its meaning are both an *effect* of context. Fail to learn the rules (i.e., context) of English and this very text is hardly something to be scanned for its meaning. Come to think of it, put a *National Geographic Magazine* or a Sears Roebuck catalogue in an outhouse a hundred years ago and it doesn't take a genius to know that they're not there to be read!

What Taylor therefore fails to see—but what is more than evident to anyone who does not share his Canadian setting—is that the joy and exultation he feels whenever a small black rubber disk crosses the other team's goal line, accompanied by a red light, a siren, and the broadcaster proclaiming, "He shoots, he scores!", are *effects* of his social world. It is therefore not that the inner emotion mutates when it is shared; the fact of having the inner emotion *is evidence of a lot of sharing having already taken place!* Surely these social effects (a.k.a. emotions) can be reinforced and thus compounded, based on such factors as whether other people are also in the room cheering, drinking beer, slapping you on the back, or, instead, impatiently trying to change the television's channel, but this does not lessen the fact that the game is *not* inherently joyous, exciting, or boring. Just because I cannot sit through an entire US college football game says little, if anything at all, about the activity; instead, it says everything about the world in which I was raised and the expectations I have learned regarding such things as how I ought to spend my time on a Saturday afternoon.

We can conclude—quoting James's own words once again but not lamenting anything, as he does—that Taylor's emotional response to the game "has been made for him by others, communicated to him by tradition, determined to fixed forms by imitation, and retained by habit." Prior to the advent of this social frame, there was no game let alone exultation and joy over how the game was played and by whom. Thus, Taylor's attempt to shift some of the weight of James's analysis from the "private breast" displaces nothing; in fact, by giving a thin social veneer to supposedly pristine inner emotions it reinscribes the priority of the stable center (call it meaning or intention) adrift in the tempestuous seas of historical change (i.e., context). Appealing to Slavoj Žižek—commenting not on moral philosophy but, instead, on the way in which seemingly oppositional, ironic, popular culture poses no opposition whatsoever—we can conclude that "through all these displacements *the same old story is being told.* In short, the true function of these displacements and subversions is precisely to make the traditional story relevant to our 'postmodern' age—and thus to prevent us from replacing it with a new narrative" (2002, 70; Žižek's emphasis). The point of Žižek's critique is the conservative function of the irony, reversals, and self-parody that are at the heart of the recent animated feature film, *Shrek* (2001), in which a seemingly beautiful princess finds love and thus turns into her true self: a green ogre. "[W]e make fun of our beliefs," he writes, "while continuing to practice them, that is, to rely on them as the underlying structure of our daily practice" (2002, 71). Just as the new and improved tale of the green ogre sells viewers the same bag of goods as did earlier fairy tales, Taylor's update is no update at all, but simply a repackaging of the same technique for sentimentalizing what might otherwise be understood as thoroughly public and therefore contestable social worlds. Such sentimentalization amounts to ahistorical obscurantism insomuch as it hides from view the haphazard manner in which one's contingent placement in a specific social world leads to differing experiences.

· With this penchant for personalizing the social in mind, and the counter effort to reinscribe experience back into history, the following essays attempt to re-inject not religion but, more importantly perhaps, the category "religion" itself back into history. Like James, I acknowledge that "religion" is equivocal, but hardly in the manner he maintained. Although it is certainly used as part of a folk taxonomy common in social worlds with which the reader is more than likely familiar (worlds in which people routinely say such things as, "I'm religious, are you?"), the fact that members of many other cultures do not classify their own worlds in this manner indicates that our folk taxonomy can also occupy our critical attention, prompting us to examine the social and political roles played by this designation *qua* social classification. The following chapters therefore attempt to unpack some of the issues involved in answering the following question: what if we approached the study of world events not with the preconceived notion that religion was essentially pure and spiritual matter of disembodied belief but, instead, with the presumption that all classification systems (such as Church vs. State, belief vs. practice and embodied vs. disembodied) are the means whereby all too historical groups negotiate—sometimes violently, always aggressively—sets of interests that determine who they think they are and who they think they are not? A shift capable of answering this question would enable us to see that, regardless by whom they are used, rhetorics of origin, privacy, authenticity, spirit, tradition, essence, faith, along with the common distinction between belief and action (seen in the common-sense distinction between myth and ritual) or content and structure, are useful (and useful to whom is the question that needs to be posed) political techniques that can help to massage and manage an unruly social world that generally does not meet with any group's expectations, interests, and needs.

Case in point: consider a recent legal episode in the US, in which a large number of Roman Catholic priests across the country have been accused of sexually abusing young boys. As reported in early March 2003, by National Public Radio's news show, "Morning Edition," the Cardinal of the Archdiocese of Los Angeles, Roger M. Mahony—whose archdiocese was at that time facing seventeen subpoenas for the disclosure of documents relating to the personnel records of current and retired priests under his direction—was "refusing to release documents that detail his communications with priests.... Lawyers for Mahony argue that private discussions between priests and their bishops are protected by the First Amendment." After all, or so the argument goes, "there is a special relationship between bishop and priest, part employer and employee, part father and adult son, part spiritual adviser and seeker, and the privacy of that relationship must be preserved," as argued the Archdiocese's spokesman Todd Tamberg.[10]

> Priests need to have a place to speak in confidence about their spiritual life, about their ongoing formation and their religious development [elaborated Tamberg]. This tradition of confidential communication, about the most intimate details of a priest's life really lies at the core of a bishop's relationship with his priests. And so that's what we're asserting as something that needs to be protected.[11]

Or, as reported in March 2003 in the *Los Angeles Times*, the Cardinal's lawyers

> are arguing that the priest-bishop confidentiality is a foundation of the Catholic religion, and that interfering in that violates the free exercise of religion. (Lobdell and Winton 2003, B1)

So, according to those defending the interests of the Cardinal, on the one hand we have special, privileged, "private pastoral conversations" that are essentially spiritual (i.e., treating "the relationship between bishops and priests *as a sacred and private one*" [Lobdell and Winton 2003, B1; emphasis added]) while, on the other, they talk about such things as "hard evidence" and the "factual information" that is available in the public domain, if only prosecutors and investigators relied on the tried and trusted methods of "old-fashioned" investigation rather than sinking so low as to issue subpoenas for what ought to be honored as private personnel files— to borrow some predictable phrases from Don Stier, the attorney who "represents about a dozen accused priests, [and who] ... strongly supports Cardinal Mahony's position." Understandably, perhaps, the lawyer for forty alleged victims disagrees with such neat and tidy dichotomies as private/ public and sacred/secular; John Manly's "perception is that they've [the Archdiocese] directly created wholesale with no basis either in canon law, church law, or American law, a privilege which doesn't exist that would effectively, if implemented, shield them from liability from everything from drunk driving to murder."

My hope is that readers see that this is not simply an idle dispute over the names that we give to real things in the world—as if a stable, external world exists regardless of the names we use to label its parts ("a rose by any other name would smell as sweet," wrote William Shakespeare in Act II of *Romeo and Juliet*). Neither is the issue whether the accused priests behaved as religious people *ought* to have behaved (however that might be), for, contrary to James, we no longer presume that there is some stable, definitive inner experience, possessed only by religious geniuses, that sets the bar by means of which we can judge the adequacy of this or that degraded imitation. Instead, we should investigate the links between such classifications as "private," "sacred," and "religious" and their relations to explicit disputes over socio-political turf and, hence, identity and the means to satisfy one's interests. After all, at the heart of the case of sexual abuse lawsuits against Roman Catholic priests is the issue of legal jurisdiction (i.e., turf!); as the old argument goes, "civil authorities don't have the constitutional right to intervene in church affairs" (Lobdell and Winton 2003, B6). In fact, in liberal democracies such as the US there is a long history of the courts *allowing* (I italicize the verb to draw attention to the fact that the public courts of the modern nation-state either *grant* or *withhold* privacy and autonomy; they do not merely *recognize* and thus *honor* it) groups designated as "religious" wide latitude in their self-policing activities, evidenced by the fact that such things as lawsuits over wrongful dismissal of ritual specialists and theologians are not as easy to deal with in the courts as they would be if such dismissals occurred in other sectors of the economy. But this autonomy (which, in the US, is at least in part a function of the way in which the Internal Revenue

Service [IRS] defines a church[12]) and the nation-state's seemingly benign tolerance of "different spheres" are short-lived when an apparently invisible, ill-defined line is crossed—in this case, the now much-valued innocence of children. For, as Asad notes, "[i]f citizens are not reasoned around in a manner deemed nationally important by the government and the majority that supports it, the threat of legal action (and the violence this implies) may be used" (2003, 6).

Learning to hear talk of religion, meaning, text, faith, experience, spirituality, intention, etc., as nothing more or less than artful social rhetorics—as modern ways of "reasoning around" the complexities and ambiguities of our daily lives—is therefore at the heart of the following chapters. A widely accepted series of oppositions is investigated as a site where generally undisclosed social work is taking place. Whether it be: the full understanding of history possible when a text is read in its proper context; the effort to bridge, and thus resolve, the gap between some supposedly uniform "past" and the present; the attempt to overcome the distance, and thus misunderstandings, between participants and non-participants; the manner in which political influence is sometimes thought to impact only institutional structures but not the intellectual content carried out at these sites; or the way in which some mass social movements are represented as having two mutually exclusive aspects: on the one hand they are seen as a peaceful, tolerant religious tradition while, on the other, they are seen to have deviant, fanatical, and sadly politicized manifestations—all of these tactical oppositions are seen as social sites where specific sorts of political work is being done through the artful deployment of distinctive sets of classifications.

But of all these categorial distinctions, one in particular attracts my attention: none other than the popular notion of the authentic origin as a site of ultimate meaning vs. our inevitably degraded forms of historical expression and practice. My hope is that readers can entertain that this distinction is doing a considerable amount of political work. For, if many writers are deeply suspicious of the terrorist/freedom fighter, and the regime/ government, distinctions that were so quickly invoked in the international debates that followed on the heels of the September 11 attacks—debates aimed at preserving the unquestionable right to use violent (yet self-righteous) conflict for "our" purposes—then why not question the utility of their own apparently common-sense authentic/inauthentic distinctions?

A final comment or two: first, careful readers will understand that, in developing the following critique, I am not trying to persuade anyone regarding what the movements classified as religion really are or how they ought to be understood—other than the fact that they are here taken to be thoroughly historical instances of contestable human behavior. So, as Donald Lopez wrote in the opening of *Prisoners of Shangri-La*—his critique of popular and scholarly representations of Tibetan Buddhism—"[t]he question to be considered is not how knowledge is tainted," as if some pristine form of knowledge emerges once it has passed through the fires of critical analysis; instead, the question is "how knowledge takes form" (1998, 13). Although his work is on the politics of images of Tibet, Lopez's words are equally applicable to the study of how representations of mass movements do or do not function in reproducing the necessary conditions of the movements themselves. So, let me repeat (borrowing Lopez's words once again, but applying them well beyond the cultures of the Himalayas): "the point is not to debunk with a catalog of facts our most cherished notions about Tibet ... to more accurately depict what Tibet was or is 'really like.' ... Nor is the point to suggest that Tibetan Buddhism is merely an instrument of oppression exercised in bad faith by power-hungry clerics. The important questions are *why* these myths persist and *how* they continue to circulate unchallenged" (p. 9).

Second, although the following is not primarily about Islam, contemporary representations of Islam are used at a number of points as a timely example of the politics of classification as it is currently being played out by scholars and politicians. In asking the reader to consider the ways in which classifications such as "religion," "faith," and "full understanding" help to make certain forms of knowledge possible—knowledge that enables some group members to channel difference and dissent into non-threatening avenues—Islam is used merely as a case study in which the practical impact of these issues is difficult to ignore. So, at least in part, the following essays benefit from the work of the late Edward Said, for they are concerned with the ways of representing mass movements in the media and in contemporary scholarship. But, pressing considerably beyond Said, the following chapters examine the utility of naming some parts of our social worlds as "religions"—and their members as uniformly "pious" and "faithful"—in distinction to other parts of those worlds that are understood as public and therefore contestable.

In the final analysis, then, this book is but the next step in a series of studies in the socio-rhetorical conditions that help to make possible the largest social formation that—for good or ill—we have so far come up with, this thing we have come to know as the modern, liberal nation-state. Because those who are interested in the study of the nation generally share the assumption that religion names a semi-autonomous, obviously existing collection of related beliefs, manifested in ritual practices and institutions that are somehow set apart from politics and which occasionally exert a political force (as in the so-called Moral Majority, the Christian Right, or that ill-defined danger that goes by the name of Fundamentalism), such scholars are not necessarily familiar with advances made in the academic study of religion—or, perhaps I should say, the academic study of the taxon "religion." They are therefore not acquainted with the ways in which discourses on religion and faith help to make possible a social site where—to borrow some phrasing from the scholar of antiquity, Peter Brown—members of groups "iron out the tensions and anomalies of real life" (2003, 18). These are rhetorics that both signal and facilitate group members becoming increasingly preoccupied with themselves *as* selves and *as* citizens and, in the process, becoming more governable due to their general absence from that contest we now term public life. For, as Michel Foucault phrased it:

> [Socrates's] mission is useful for the city—more useful than the Athenians' military victory at Olympia—because in teaching people to occupy themselves with themselves, he teaches them to occupy themselves with the city.... I think that the main characteristic of our political rationality is the fact that this integration of the individuals in a community or in a totality results from a constant correlation between an increasing individualization and the reinforcement of this totality. (Foucault 1988, 20, 161–62)

I used this very quotation as the epigraph of the final chapter of my previous book, *The Discipline of Religion*. Insomuch as this brief book is aimed to advance the analysis with which that book ended, it is only fitting, then, that I re-use these lines, but this time to provide an opening rather than an ending.

2 Swapping Spit Around the Camp Fire

My wife and I once worked as Dons (what in the US might be termed a Resident Advisor) in a co-ed residence at the University of Toronto's University College. One of the building's porters, a older gentleman named Carl who has since died, worked the afternoon shift. Originally from somewhere in what we once called Eastern Europe, he had fought in World War II, for various armies. As one was defeated by another, a number of soldiers simply changed sides, took up with their new compatriots, and kept on going; after all, the alternative was more than likely not nearly as appealing.

Late one evening while on his nightly rounds, he came upon a small group of undergraduate students in one of the dimly lit common rooms, confessing to one another their past misdeeds: the curfews they had missed and their high-school drinking-binges. Stopping for a moment, I was told the next morning how the porter had stood just outside their circle and listened. Turning to him, a young student invited Carl to divulge one of his own past infractions. Because he was old enough to be the students' great-grandfather, more than likely they all anticipated hearing some quaint, antique recollection—a confession that would enable the old man to join yet another new group of compatriots.

Instead of offering a familiar tale about the "good ole days," Carl replied in his thickly accented English:

"In zee var ve vould burn Polish villages."

In the complete silence that greeted his disclosure—calling his words a confession entirely misses the point of this anecdote—he turned, and, as it was told to me, walked back into the darkness to continue his rounds, having declined the invitation to join at least this one group.

Whenever I think of scholars and educated commentators dutifully working to identify the pristine center that can speak authoritatively for and to the proverbial Other, so as to bring about mutual understanding and thus tolerance, I cannot help but recall the porter walking out of the room after having upped the ante considerably. For those upper-middle-class students were completely unprepared to entertain anyone's world as being so far removed from their own that Carl's story would be anything other than sneaking out of his room late one evening to meet a young lady. In the same manner that their late-night confessions—much like telling scary tales around a camp fire—functioned to unite them by reinforcing the boundaries of the expected and the allowable, their dumbfounded reaction to the porter's report, recounted with no hint of shame or irony, makes apparent the parochial nature of the preferences that—prior to hearing his tale, that is—they had taken for granted as universal and self-evident.

Such moments therefore remind me of the inevitably local and self-serving nature of all forms of in-group story-telling that presume to exist some stable center that is set apart from the interest-ladened, contingent, and potentially contradictory perspectives of competing historical agents. This is none other than the ideology of closure that sometimes goes by the name of the insider/outsider problem.[1] But this so-called problem of trying to mediate between and thus minimize the effects of differing commitments is a problem only for those motivated by the wishful hope that there somewhere exists a detached, god's-eye viewpoint from which the entire pachyderm of human meaning can somehow be experienced by carefully listening to the tales of the proverbial blind men. If this is indeed the case, if there *is* some big picture that we will recognize only after a considerable amount of inductive data gathering—and how to demonstrate its existence is, of course, the $64,000 question—then I can at least understand what compels some to presume that we all have a story to tell and thus all deserve our fifteen minutes of fame; but if there is no such beast, if the blind men are truly blind, groping without the benefit of the omniscient narrator who is required to make that proverb work, then we are disingenuous in inviting everyone to tell their story, for I suspect that—like those students in my anecdote—we are not all prepared to listen patiently and appreciatively to everyone who might come out of the darkness, espousing their deeply held beliefs.

To begin to understand the problems with this problem we should first note that there are many academic fields in which there is nothing equivalent to the insider/outsider problem that some people use to mediate between what might otherwise be understood as a cacophony of competing voices. These are fields in which writers feel no guilt when they offer analyses that use participant disclosures as data that is then subjected to theoretical analysis. In once comparing the scholar of religion to the doctor whose efforts to understand the workings of the human body require no input whatsoever from the comatose patient, Robert Segal, of Lancaster University, once took an obviously provocative stand on this issue, one seldom adopted by scholars of religion for fear of offending the people whom we study. That some members of the audience at the conference in Mexico City where he struck upon this analogy were, to put it mildly, aghast suggests that the study of religion is not one of the fields that somehow escapes the insider/outsider problem.[2] But why is this?

The common answer draws on Wilhelm Dilthey's (1833–1911) sharp split between the so-called sciences of the spirit and those of nature. Insomuch as humans are thought to possess independent consciousness, we are free, moral beings. Therefore, unlike the predictable behavior of physical objects, the study of human beliefs and actions must necessarily take into account the intentional ghost inhabiting the physical machine. An objective "science of man" was therefore seen by some as demeaning insomuch as it placed people on a par with unthinking objects. As recently quoted by Faydra Shapiro, of Wilfrid Laurier University, in an article on the intersection between ethnography and autobiography:

> In trying to become "objective" Western culture made "objects" of things and people when it distanced itself from them, thereby losing "touch" with them. This dichotomy is the root of all violence. (2003, 193, quoting Anzaldua 1987, 37)

Because human beings are thought to *act*, rather than simply *behave*, their actions must be understood as part of a larger system of meanings. Accordingly, the study of these actions must be interpretive, not explanatory, and the participant's understanding of his or her own motivations and meanings enters a dialogue with the understandings of the observer—otherwise, or so it is said, scholars will do violence to the dignity of the person under study, not to mention jeopardizing their own humanity as well.

Even if we grant this division of labor—and let me add that it is far from obvious that we ought to!—the traditional split between the sorts of objects under study (e.g., people versus things) and the methods used in their study (e.g., interpretation versus explanation) does not really help to account for why *only some* intellectual pursuits worry so much over having the scholar keep in touch with the participant by having them exchange self-disclosures, much as symbolic gifts are exchanged whenever we try to forge new friendships. It does not help because, as made plain in the story of Carl and the students, we likely don't want to be friends with everyone and therefore we'd better be a little more explicit about how we choose our dance partners.

But so long as we keep dancing with people who already know *our* steps by heart, we really don't have to be very articulate about when we do and do not make our own personal disclosures, for we likely make them all the time and never need make apologies for it. And whenever someone steps on someone else's toes while doing this consensual dance, then they can always just invoke the insider/outsider problem to finesse the misstep (that is, to solve the problem of misunderstanding). Does this help us to understand why we would never expect to see a book entitled something like *The Insider/Outsider Problem in the Study of Ancient Athens*, or *The Insider/Outsider Problem in the Study of Nazism*?[3] Why are such titles not on our library shelves? (Just who constitutes this "our" might provide the answer to this question.) Well, in the case of the first the answer is easy: there are no ancient Athenians to interview (i.e., participant-observation is an impossibility in this case, so worrying over how best to do it is irrelevant);

moreover, anyone trying to recover some sort of authentic Athenianness is hopelessly left with the modern problem of leaping across great divides in the interpretation of ancient artifacts—an all too contemporary activity; despite the apparent antiquity of any text, it is always in the present, in front of the eyes of a modern reader who, by some imaginative act, must conjure up a dimly lit past despite never leaving the here-and-now.

With this imaginative leap in mind, I recall how, as a young boy, I once learned to spread butter over paper on which I had drawn something (say, a copy of one of Leonardo da Vinci's sketches, because they already looked old and authentic), tear the page's borders to make it look tattered, and then bake it at a low temperature to make it look old. Despite the fact that the crisp, yellowed paper that emerged from the hot oven was, in fact, newer than the one that had gone in just a few minutes before, it took on the aura of antiquity that its precursor could never have possessed. Despite their not using butter, this strikes me as an apt analogy for the imaginative aging in which scholars who read "ancient documents" regularly engage. But despite their best efforts to closely read flimsy fragments with white gloves, tweezers, and a reverential attitude they fall considerably short of the kind of time travel needed to provide an unimpeded access to some posited *ancien mentalité*. Commenting on the early role the science of bibliography once played in the hopeful efforts of some to reconstruct the original and thus uniform Shakespearean text (and hence the original and uniform Shakespearean intention and thus his text's enduring meaning), the Princeton historian, Robert Darnton, has recently phrased it as follows:

> Textual conundrums ... inspired generations of scholars to feats of ever-greater virtuosity. By poring over early editions, they have traced typographical clues over every variety—inconsistent spelling, irregularities in spacing, chipped type, anything that could help them reconstruct the production processes of Elizabethan printing shops and therefore get closer to Shakespeare's missing copy. Many learned to set type themselves and turned into amateur letterpress printers. In their imaginations, Ph.D.s became companions of the workers who first turned Shakespeare's words into books. It was an intoxicating idea, and it did not last. (2003b, 43)[4]

That such intoxicating yet, in the final analysis, utterly unproductive attempts to recover ancient intentions and authentic meanings continue to be widely shared by colleagues from across the disciplines—not least by some of those who yet study the Bible so as to figure out what the historical Jesus really said—should not go unnoticed. Despite the confidence they have in the contexts they have recovered, into which they faithfully read their text to find its enduring meaning, the historical conundrums yet persist.

The conundrums persist because, when talking about the past of any item, there is a problem with trying to identify "*its* history" and "*its* context." Here, history is the object that is thought to be possessed by some stable subject, say, a piece of broken clay—*its* history apparently stretches backward, in a linear series of cause-effect relationships, from the shard-in-the-present into the dimly lit past, much like the train on an elegant wedding dress or the wake from a passing ship. But who (other than a fool or an ardent philosophical idealist) would doubt that the clay fragment has a past? Recovering this history means working backward, from a fragment along the linear time line to some posited pristine whole (i.e., the original, unblemished pot), to answer such questions as "How was *it* (i.e., the pot that sat long ago, at the originary point of our time line) broken?" But we must keep in mind that only the clay fragment (even "fragment" presupposes a referential point that is whole and complete) is contemporaneous with the person who poses this question, who has this particular curiosity, and that the "it" (i.e., the thing of which our clay is thought to be but a fragment) is necessarily a discursive figment of one's imagination. In other words, if we can at least agree, for the time being, that the clay shard is an empirical item in the inter-subjective world that we can observe, then the ancient pot is forever an item of discourse.[5] This is overlooked, however, in framing the issue in terms of the clay fragment's history (noting, once again, the possessive). It is crucial to note that, for the scholar who takes seriously the contingent nature of this thing we generalize as historical existence, all of human history has not aimed at producing the chip from the long lost whatever-it-was, let alone producing the curiosity that drives our search for the clumsy oaf who must have dropped it, or the cattle that stepped on it, or the shifting tectonic plates that tumbled it.

The problem, then, is that the view of history or context *qua* possession necessarily leaves unquestioned the *choice* that is exercised in setting the table with a particular zenith point or a target (i.e., our clay fragment). Yet this very item is the choice of an actor (the archeologist, perhaps?) whose very existence, let alone his or her curiosities and choices, is inevitably but one more part of contingent history, making the broken piece of clay *qua* item of inquiry but an arbitrary (but no less interesting) node that—given other interests, other curiosities, etc.—could just as easily have been an old pipe, or an oak barrel, or a dirty handkerchief, iron manufacturing trends in nineteenth-century Britain, cotton harvest yields in the pre-Civil War US South, etc.

Given just how rich and varied the past more than likely was, an additional problem arises for efforts to recover the proper historical context of some object: much of the past is an utter mystery due to the fact that it is unrecoverably lost or never was recorded to begin with. While I would like to say "most" of the past has been lost, since we do not have access to a vantage point that would allow us to see history in its entirety, we cannot even make this comparative judgement with any degree of certainty. As applied to the problem of recovering an historical context within which to place artifacts in need of interpretation, contemporary scholars lack any standard by which to judge when a sufficient amount of context has been collected, in terms of which the text can be placed to judge its meaning, original use, intended effect, etc. Much as with any conclusion based on inductive reasoning, all historical judgements must therefore be offered as tentative conclusions whose persuasiveness is premised not on their ability to fit the facts of history (since we'll never know when we've seen the last spotted dog so as to make certain our claim regarding "All dogs have spots"); instead, persuasiveness is based on the manner in which our claims about the past conform to (and thereby confirm) a set of practices by means of which the past becomes an item of contemporary discourse.

If not the possession of a stable present boldly moving forward along a linear path, then what does "history" or "context" designate? When it comes to talking about history, there is no definitive past of which we can speak, and no definite context, just a host of competing pasts, most of which have been utterly and unrecoverably lost since they have left no empirical trace (or, at least none that catch our interest); there are only a host of competing items that can be isolated, by means of contemporary standards, as "texts," a host of competing elements that can be assembled, by means of contemporary standards, into "contexts" to serve virtually any number of competing interests. Much as the nineteenth-century's notion of "society" in the singular was long ago identified as problematic, "history" and "context" in the singular can even be part of the conundrum, for all that we have are histories and contexts that are composed by actors with various practical, social interests that are all placed firmly in the present, all of whom are working with the benefit of selective hindsight to identify, prune, and thereby normalize but one particular set of relations that will help them to create settings into which they can place (i.e., make sense of) a specific present and thereby make possible an anticipated future. Accordingly, "the past" is a shorthand for the innumerable past occurrences that, from this or that vantage point, can be connected (or discounted) in a series of virtually infinite variations to arrive at infinitely different presents and infinitely varied speculative endpoints.

The past *qua* possession (i.e., the clay's history, as well as a text's context) thus fails to take seriously that the present, or a group's asserted identity, or the meaning of a text is not some teleological endpoint to which a stable development has moved, much like the beast who "slouches toward Bethlehem, to be born," in W. B. Yeat's famous poem, "The Second Coming" (1916); history and context are not what a thing possesses; instead, history and context *qua* a series of narrative connections in the present, that are prompted by a particular set of curiosities and interests, enables some mundane thing (what the anthropologist Mary Douglas once referred to as "matter" or what I like to name "stuff") to stand out as an item of discourse.

In this regard, things do not *have* a history or a context but, instead, histories and contexts *make* things! Therefore, talk of the past leaving its trace or leaving evidence is highly misleading for it conjures up the image of a purposeful and stable baton of identity and significance being steadily passed forward, hand over hand, into the present and onward toward some already forming future. Instead, history as contingency had no intentions and did not leave anything to us; instead, the present is a site cluttered with objects, only some of which will get to count as so-called artifacts—or, better yet, relics—as opposed to "junk" or merely the more neutral "stuff." Accordingly, stuff becomes a relic only once it is placed by an actor within a series of specific narrative connections—insomuch as it becomes an item of discourse.

History, therefore, is posited in the following essay as an open-ended domain that stretches outward indefinitely from innumerable present moments; much like Yeat's free-wheeling falcon who cannot hear his falconer, localized at each of these nodes of history is an ever widening gyre into which we can read any number of possible pasts and hoped for/dreaded futures. The conundrum, then, is that "the past" is an infinitely useful yet utterly speculative discursive domain; it is a repository of signifiers that are all in the present but which acquire their supposed antiquity from being used to project current interests outward, thereby ensuring that they are understood as eternal, uniform, and thus self-evident and beyond debate. And, much like that powerless falconer, it is the wishful historian who attempts to regulate the essentially untamed economy of signification (a term I continually borrow from Jonathan Z. Smith), to control it, and ensure that "the past" as Other includes only what we want it to, helping us to forget the many other moments that were once competitors for our attention.

But, appealing to Yeats's once again, despite our best efforts to manage it, to create a definitive center to which everything is tethered—whether that center is the scholar of religion's "the sacred," the biologist's "laws of nature," the "invisible hand" of economists, or the liberal humanist's "human nature"—the infinitely varied pasts, thoroughly competitive interests, and endlessly malleable identities ensure that:

> Things fall apart; the centre cannot hold;
> Mere anarchy is loosed upon the world ...
> *The Second Coming*, 1916

Or at least those working to normalize but one past, one identity, one center, might say as much. Yet, contrary to this lament, every artifact, every relic, every text, every piece of evidence is therefore unwieldy since it has innumerable—some of which are surely conflicting and many of which are forever lost—possible referents and potential significations. The past *qua* item of discourse is therefore akin to the "date" written along the bottom of the image on this book's cover: *"Muse Inquietanti"* ("The Disquieting Muses," first painted sometime around 1917), an oil painting by the Greek-born Italian artist Giorgio de Chirico (1888–1978) who was part of the so-called anti-rational art movement in Italian art (or what he termed *pittura metafisica* [metaphysical painting]). For it may very well be a mistake to think this number corresponds to a date casually signed on the canvas as an after-thought (or placed after an author's name in a text such as the one just above) rather than viewing it as part of the artwork itself; various copies of this painting exist, all dated, by art historians, to the years between 1917 and 1947, prompting us to see the "date" as part of the art that de Chirico apparently copied faithfully across a thirty-year period, leaving nearly twenty copies of the painting (or is each an original?). With René Magritte's famous painting, "Ceçi n'est pas une pipe" (1926; see Foucault 1973) in mind, we might reasonably conclude that the often occurring brush strokes in the painting's lower left corner *are not either a date or a number.* They're art![6]

Copy-making, like meaning-making and identity-making, is therefore the skill of those who use conventions to domesticate unruly collections of significations. Only if we presuppose de Chirico's chronologically first canvas was somehow the *Ur*-text, the original embodiment of something we can simply call inspiration (akin to William James's notion of charisma and genius), would there be anything to gain by going down the trail in hot pursuit of the artist's original intention, chasing it much like Darnton's Shakespearean bibliographers, all in an effort to cut through a host of extraneous historical accumulations. However, if we presume instead that each canvas, each distinct practice, is an instance of utilizing conventions for possibly changing effect, then we will see that the conundrums associated with searching for the original and therefore authentic historical intention of some ancient Athenian, for example, is akin to Alice falling down the rabbit hole.

As for the second hypothetical title mentioned above—*The Insider/ Outsider Problem in the Study of Nazism*—it is likely inconceivable for scholars in modern, liberal democracies to entertain that their adversaries have a legitimate opinion about themselves and their motives that is worth sharing as part of an ongoing conversation—and by "legitimate" I simply mean one that is seen to compete with, complement, or enhance the scholar's own analysis. In fact, entertaining any of these options would, more than likely, be judged as an immoral stand, perhaps prompting some to accuse us of a seditious act of treason. Although it would be easy to draw on a contemporary example—say, the manner in which so-called Islamic fanatics' explanations for their own violent actions are dismissed as lies, delusions, or double-speak in need of careful decoding (making those who fail to question the epistemic status of these reports "mere pawns in the terrorists' hands")—consider the case of the one-time Nazi Minister of Armaments and War Production and so-called "architect of the Third

Reich," Albert Speer (1905–81)—one of the few defendants to plead guilty at the Nuremberg trials and who served twenty years in Spandau prison, in what was once East Berlin, until his release on October 1, 1966. His memoirs (Speer 1970; see also his prison diaries [Speer 1976]) hold a celebrated status for scholars insomuch as Speer's recorded self-disclosures about the war years are understood to be an example of an astute political actor, working with the benefit of hindsight, to rationalize his own actions and thereby fool his obviously culpable self and his unwary readers alike! (Regarding scholarship on Speer's memoirs, see such works as Fest 2001, Hauerwas 1977, Sereny 1995, van der Zant 1997.) Such an insider's self-report is therefore not part of an ongoing conversation with the scholar; instead, it is of interest only insomuch as it is understood either as an example of self-delusion, outright lying, or evidence of the reporter apologizing for his past misdeeds.

Whether or not one agrees with how such scholars have used Speer's memoirs, we must at least note that their goal is not to avoid doing violence to the integrity of an author's efforts to "describe the past as I experienced it" (as quoted in Speer's foreword)—as if participants set the bar for how their behaviors can be understood and redescribed by scholars. Instead of trying to sympathize with, empathize with, or protect his authorial voice and his right to interpret his own experiences, their goal is to explain *why* someone as seemingly well educated and cultured as Speer would understand his own behavior in a way that differs so dramatically from how we understand it.[7] Because we have such confidence in the superiority of our own systems of morality and our own understanding of history, no apologies are needed when our conclusions regarding self-deception trump Speer's protestations of his youthful political *naïveté*.

It would appear, then, that we have no need of mediating between competing disclosures and commitments when we study our enemies, for they are deluded, lying, sinful, or brainwashed, and only we are able to cut through the ideology to intuit the heart of the matter. So the question arises: when does the scholarly suspension of first-person interpretive authority (i.e., the right to interpret and express one's own motives and meanings) qualify as an instance of epistemic violence and when does a *failure* to suspend the participant's own interpretive authority amount to an offensive or immoral act? To rephrase: when do Others have an authentic inner core which they rightfully express, and which we seek to integrate into our ever growing understanding of human nature, and when do we judge these expressions to be evidence of a core that has gone rotten?

To answer my own question, it strikes me that the so-called insider/outsider problem is an opportunity for mediating between conflicts, and thereby achieving mutual understanding, only when the observer has some sort of affinity for the behaviors under study. When addressing those beliefs and behaviors with which we disagree, we lose no sleep whatsoever when we offer an analysis that contradicts participants' own self-understandings and suspends their right to add their voice to our conversation. For instance, pick up virtually any study of a group—other than our own, of course—that resorts to violence to accomplish its political and economic goals and, despite the best intentions of the empathetic commentator, the point of studying them is not to be in touch with these people by conversing with them and keeping in touch with their deep commitments. Sooner or later the other shoe drops when the writer adopts an explanatory framework in order to determine *why anyone would do such a thing.*

I therefore see scholarship *qua* conversation among equals, scholarship seen as an opportunity for making collegial disclosures of personal commitments, as having profound political ramifications that are spelled out in the following chapters; for the time being, suffice it to mark them as a social engineering technique used by specific groups to establish tactical coalitions by selectively smoothing over what, for the purpose of some anticipated coalition, are perceived to be relatively minor material differences submerged within an essential, nonempirical similarity, all in an effort to circle the wagons against the onslaught of the significant material differences that threaten some apparent "us" and "our" interests. Recognizing and then trying to address seemingly competing commitments therefore arises only when an empirically diverse and possibly conflicting "many" is, for whatever reason, presumed by its members to be subordinated to a common unity (call it human nature, nationality, religious experience, gender, ethnicity, freedom, or the free market). That this triumphant oneness, achieved by means of establishing mutual understanding, turns out to be anything but an inclusive conversation must not go unnoticed.

For instance, consider how all of this works in a recent British collection of essays entitled *Theorizing Faith: The Insider/Outsider Problem in the Study of Ritual.* The various chapters in this book—on such marginal groups as British Muslims, Soka Gakkai in the UK, British Quakerism, and British Wicca—set about addressing the practical problems posed by difference by presuming—unlike Speer's learned commentators—that there exists some "big picture" to which participants *and* observers alike have limited yet complementary access. This is phrased in the book's conclusion as follows:

> All of this is rooted in an epistemology ... in which no single "voice" has the capacity for the whole truth, but in which every voice is a potential source of fact and insight, and in which valid conclusions and adequate interpretations are more likely, when the multiple voices are sensitively heard and considered.... If we can build multiple perspectives into our research project, whether through team research in the field, sharing at conferences, or other forms of collegial discourse, we are blessed. (Arweck and Stringer 1999, 159)

The unelaborated qualifications that lead to this blessed event surely deserve some attention, for they provide such writers with considerable wiggle-room to accomplish two crucial things: (i) to avoid sanctioning the wrong voices and (ii) to keep anyone from noticing that they avoid sanctioning the wrong voices—in this manner we can feel rather good about how inclusive our circle is, all the while hearing comforting stories that we already know by heart, for the conventions that determine the form our conversation takes preclude the wrong voices and surprising stories from ever gaining entry.

Because of the inclusivity rhetoric there can be no voice that is excluded, so we need to come up with classifications to name the wrong voices as something other than voices. I am reminded here of an aside made on April 9, 2003, by a cable news commentator as the television news cameras zoomed in on the toppling of the statue of Saddam Hussein, on the day that US troops first arrived in Baghdad. One of the risks of bringing democracy to Iraq, the pundit said, was that they might elect the wrong government. More than likely this remark went unnoticed to the majority of viewers, since we all pretty much know what the wrong government is—they're the ones we call regimes because they don't have our best interests at heart. His comment went unnoticed, that is, until his colleague observed that in a democracy there's no such thing as electing the wrong government. *Touché.*

Usually, though, no one plays the role of referee and calls us on how our efforts to hear all of the voices inevitably slip into a self-interested monologue. After all, as made plain in the above indented quotation, every voice is merely a *potential* source of fact and insight; conclusions can be either *valid* or *invalid* while interpretations can either be *adequate* or *inadequate*; we are told that, as listeners, we must be *sensitive* and our discourse must be *collegial*; otherwise, I presume, we are not allowed to play the game. All too predictably, however, we find no argumentation in favor of any criteria whereby, for instance, valid from invalid conclusions can be distinguished and no suggestion as to what constitutes a collegial discourse. This should be enough to cause the wary reader to pause, especially those acquainted with the ways in which the category "collegiality" is sometimes used in the academy to assert some rather unprofessional criteria that determine one's inclusion within the guild.

This presumption that our criteria are self-evident and universal—something most people share with the students in this chapter's opening anecdote—is evidence of a nostalgia for the innocence that comes with full understanding—a nostalgia for some posited totality that is greater than the sum of its individual and seemingly conflicting parts. It is a profoundly anti-historical attitude that strikes me as most troublesome in the writings of those working to mediate between differing viewpoints and commitments. For, instead of presuming that historical existence is shot through and through with competing interests, the rhetoric of "full understanding" that propels the desire to keep in touch with (just some of) the people we study and which prompts some of us to think that all so-called deeply held beliefs can find a place at the table, bypasses the requirements (and thus the risks) of public persuasion; in bypassing these requirements it shows itself to be based on anything but a humble epistemological foundation. Instead, it provides a passive/aggressive means to portray some local as the self-evident universal without ever really considering that interests and viewpoints might be incommensurable or contradictory. I think here of Jonathan Kirsch's recent book, *The Woman Who Laughed at God: The Untold History of the Jewish People* (2001), which stands as a useful example of a writer coming to grips with the fact that, at least in the case of Judaism, the only so-called core value is diversity and disagreement. Thus, all we seem to have is a host of differing Judaisms all talking *with* each other. But in making this seemingly insightful observation, we find a subtle argument that naturalizes but one sort of liberal Judaism as opposed to the many other contenders for normative status. In other words, the old "unity in diversity" nugget is a political rhetoric doing its own sort of group building in competition with other mutually exclusive conceptions of the group, some of which don't particularly want to gain entry into the big tent and don't wish to talk *with* anyone else.[8]

This rhetoric of the big picture, the unity that encompasses all diversity, the synthesis that unites all opposites, in which one attempts to attain full understanding by listening carefully to all of the voices, may be one of the most powerful political techniques we've yet come up with to silence just some voices while amplifying others. For, as phrased in a rhetorical question posed by Slavoj Žižek in his critique of the popular film, *The Matrix*: "What if ideology resides in the very belief that outside the closure of the finite universe, there is some 'true reality' to be entered?" (2001, 214). For, as afficionados of this film will recall, outside the seemingly never-ending yet only virtually real matrix is a really real world—what Žižek characterizes as "the pre-modern notion of 'arriving at the end of the universe'" (p. 215). But rather than being as subversive as many of its fans understood it to be, it is a film informed only by what the late French social theorist, Pierre Bourdieu, once termed radical chic which accomplishes apparent subversion (1998, 137). Accordingly, the "problem with the film," according to Žižek, is that "it is *not* 'crazy' enough.... Much more subversive than this multiplication of virtual universes would have been the multiplication of realities themselves" (p. 217).

Translated into the topic at hand, the far more radical way to examine the issue of differing commitments is to take seriously that there is no level playing field and, therefore, no resolution through mutual understanding to be had; the task of scholarship, then, is to recognize that the desire for dialogue is based on the old inductivist fallacy: because we'll never exhaust the voices to be heard (since the past and current social life is infinitely variable), adding our own to the mix accomplishes nothing. Instead, we need to determine some defensible principle of selection, some criterion of focus suitable to the institutions in which we do our labors, to determine how it is that we will look into the issue of difference and what will get to count as a difference worth looking into—which is simply a paraphrase of what Jonathan Z. Smith has already said:

> The questions of comparison are questions of judgment with respect to difference: What differences are to be maintained in the interests of comparative inquiry? What differences can be defensibly relaxed and relativized in light of the intellectual tasks at hand? (Smith 1987, 14; see also 1990, 47–53)

What Bruce Lincoln once termed sentiments of affinity and estrangement (1989, 10)[9] therefore ought not to function as our scholarly criteria of selection; our role as scholars ought not to be that of nurturing identification with our objects of study through entering a dialogue with them about our deepest dreams and our ultimate concerns. With this, I return to the opening anecdote: as laudable as it may seem to invite others to leave the darkness and join our circle—and who but an uncivilized brute would be against romantically swapping spit around the glowing camp fire that we euphemistically call free market, liberal democracy?—we cannot forget that huddling in our circle is not the only game in town. Moreover, I am at a loss to find anything other than self-serving rationalizations for why some social groups gain admission to *our* civil conversation—and, being our discourse, following our rules, it is duplicitous to portray it as a collaboration[10]— whereas those with whom we have limited affinity, those with whom we are in outright competition, become the objects of everything from derision to state-sponsored coercive violence. Are they just so obviously wrong that we need no rationale or persuasive reason for excluding them from the big conversation? Are their interests so out of sync with reality that we need not acknowledge that our so-called dialogue efficiently reproduces our local interests under the guise of multivocality?

Sadly, such topics are never investigated in our efforts to hear everyone's story; they are never discussed because of the classification "religion" itself. For, unlike the novice students who unknowingly invited a bull into their fledgling identity's china shop, "religion" is evidence that the easy and familiar cases of meaning-making and identity-construction have been pre-selected, enabling us to converse only with those who already qualify as "civil," "faithful," "tolerant," "sensitive," and "collegial," thereby placing on the table personal commitments that never offend us. Case in point, consider one of the positions outlined in a recent conference I attended: some argue that it is crucial to bring the students' and professor's own personal commitments into the classroom. So long as they're the "right" commitments, this is fine, of course. But what if they are not? Consider a film often used in introductory world religions classes over the past twenty-five years, *Footprint of the Buddha* (from the well-known "Long Search" series[11]): there is a scene in which Sri Lankan laywomen are wildly possessed by spirits as the local Buddhist shrine priest authenticates their possession by hitting them and splashing them in the face with water; anyone even partially familiar with the contemplative Buddhism of our textbooks, or anyone sensitive to gender relations, will immediately recognize that this is just the wrong sort of commitment. Where are the Five Noble Truths? Where is the sedate lifestyle that looks beyond appearances and slowly sips tea while commenting on the beauty of the bowl? Or consider how, beginning on September 12, 2001, the pundits began working in earnest to distance so-called authentic Islam—the "enduring values" found in the "heart of Islam" (e.g., Naasr 2002) that comprise timeless "principles" communicated by means of an apparently uniform thing we call "tradition"—from those accused of carrying out the previous day's attacks (more on this below). Is it merely a coincidence that authentic Islam ended up looking an awful lot like yet another personal choice in the free market? As phrased by one such commentator: "The challenge of the future can only be faced by an Islamic worldview that embraces diversity, equality of the sexes, and the freedom, not only to be right, but also to be wrong"—so writes Vincent Cornell, himself a Muslim and the Director of the King Fahd Center for Middle East and Islamic Studies at the University of Arkansas, in a post-September 11 essay collection entitled *Dissent from the Homeland*. "Failure to meet the challenges of a diverse, multicentered, and religiously pluralistic world," he adds, "will ultimately lead to an Islam that is irrelevant to contemporary life, and might even herald the decline of Islam as a world religion" (2003, 93). After all, as he concludes: "People who appear uncivilized do not get invited into the community of nations" (p. 92).

As with the useful rhetoric of "collegiality"—useful to tenured professors keeping their cards close to the chest when making tenure and promotion decisions, that is—such writers do not need to define just what gets to count as "right," "wrong," "relevant," "civilized," or "community;" for those of us huddled around the camp fire—those who are members in good standing of the "community of nations"—already know what they are. Much like indecency, although we couldn't actually define the limits of each of these if we had to, we apparently know once the rules have been overstepped—as did approximately 200,000 people complaining to the US's Federal Communications Commission (FCC) about the liberties Justin Timberlake and Janet Jackson took in January 2004 with what I gather are the normally family-values nature of Super Bowl halftime shows. As this recent episode makes clear, anyone who deviates too far from our unarticulated script will suffer consequences—either symbolic or material.[12]

On the wider social stage, trespassers are classified, studied, and silenced as radicals, militants, extremists, and tribalists who belong to movements that are comprised of agitators and people with strident voices who are led by belligerent leaders—to borrow a few of the terms used by the well-known liberal inclusivist, the historian of US religion Martin Marty, in his book on pluralism, *The One and the Many: America's Struggle for the Common Good* (1997) to brand those who are bold enough to put into practice their own thoughts on the common good.

To sum up, we can draw on the work of the French political theorist Dominique Colas, who was himself commenting on the political utility of the slippery rhetorics of "civil society" and "fanatic," and conclude that seeing scholarship as a place where we share personal disclosures and work toward massaging difference and establishing mutual understandings is a political problem because it "tends to present political issues as problems of management rather than as conflicts between various powers and groups with divergent or antagonistic interests" (1997, 40). And it is precisely the limits of meaning and social identity that we are attempting to manage with our efforts to converse with just some others—efforts that presume an enduring presence and deep truth that only we recognize and are able to use to ensure specific groups remain within our arm's reach while others are kept securely at arm's length.

If this is not apparent yet, then let me quote from Colas once again, to persuade readers that

> [t]he politics of presence, the quest for authenticity in the form of an immediate encounter with the real as truth, has taken quite varying forms, but they all have in common a critique of political institutions based on delegation, spokespersons, mandate-holders, representatives. The iconoclastic will to denounce political representation as imposture can no more found a politics than realism in painting can found an aesthetics. It can only give way to the same dangerous disgust with the political that seizes the fanatic each time he thinks it possible to bring forth, without delay, the kingdom of God on earth. (Colas 1997, xxx)

This is precisely why scholarly studies that seek the goal of conversation, dialogue, self-expression, and mutual understanding are entirely suspect: they reproduce and aggressively police a set of undisclosed boundaries under the guise of egalitarianism, yet because they are undisclosed (and much like standards of decency), they can conveniently be shifted to suit ever-changing interests and historical circumstances. Those who advocate such a position leave their descriptive data untheorized and, leaving it untheorized, they implicitly reinforce the object of study's status as self-evidently meaningful and sensible. Now, by "theorize" I simply mean studying all human artifacts, such as participant self-reports, as instances of data in need of historicization and explanatory analysis, and not simply appreciation or dismissal, for the task of scholarship is not to be "in touch" with the people under study, not to validate them or to pompously feel their pain, whether or not one has affinity for them.[13] Failing to subject the descriptive data to theoretical analysis results in simply adopting uncritically someone else's view of themselves and their place within their world. Then, so long as it complements or enhances our own interests, we merely perpetuate it uncritically by offering our own story that serves merely as a repetition of what the participants have already said for themselves. Despite the apparently good intentions that inspire those who seek to be "in touch" with the people they study, scholarship as repetition strikes me as chauvinistic insomuch as it presumes that what the speakers have already said for themselves requires the intellectual's authorization.

Because the intellectual's responsibility is first and foremost to that circle of wagons called the discourse of academia, there is an option for a more humble project for scholarship on human behaviors. As phrased by Jack Lightstone—a scholar of Greco-Roman Judaism who, as far back as 1984 made it evident that he had carefully read Jonathan Z. Smith—one of the basic rules that such an epistemologically modest study follows is that

> the scholar's own (analytic) *taxa* must be other than those of the data. To wholly adopt the subjects' classifications, unable to move beyond them in acts of interpretation, is to become a member of the group, bound by its framework. (Lightstone 1984, 5)

Although scholars study all sorts of human behaviors, that they do *not* speak the same language as the people they study, that they do *not* snuggle up to just anyone, is precisely the point that ought to attract our attention, prompting us to be curious about why some scholars encourage us to enter conversations about personal commitments with our research subjects rather than practicing what the University of Michigan's Tomoko Masuzawa terms "rigorous historical discourse analysis" (2000a, 164). In trying to minimize difference and conflict by presuming our identification with just some of the possible pasts and some of the self-reports we study—those we take to embody some deep, defining essence that defies historical accidents—scholars miss an ideal opportunity to make a significant contribution to just such a rigorous, cross-cultural study, one that will tell us much about how uncertain and contestable social boundaries are managed.

And so it is with this more modest goal in mind that we move on to consider the political implications of the discourse on principle, faith, essence, origin, privacy, and, finally, religion, by citing the last of Bruce Lincoln's provocative "Theses on Method":

> When one permits those whom one studies to define the terms in which they will be understood, suspends one's interest in the temporal and contingent, or fails to distinguish between "truths," "truth-claims," and

"regimes of truth," one has ceased to function as historian or scholar. In that moment, a variety of roles are available: some perfectly respectable (amanuensis, collector, friend, and advocate), and some less appealing (cheerleader, voyeur, retailer of impart goods). None, however, should be confused with scholarship. (1996, 227)

3   The Tricks and Treats of Classification

Given that an estimated 30,000 Russians die of alcohol poisoning each year (a statistic reported in Erofeyev 2002, 56), it is somewhat difficult to understand why anyone would disagree with Mikhail Gorbachev's judgement that "vodka has done more harm than good to the Russian people."[1] Instead, Evgeny Popov—a contemporary Russian author—was recently quoted, in an article on the history of the 500-year-old, odorless, colorless, and tasteless drink, to believe nonetheless that it has performed a crucial social function.

> Vodka has provided access to a private life that is closed to the state, a place where it is possible to relax, to forget your troubles, to engage in sex with the illusion of free choice. (Quoted in Erofeyev 2002, 61)

Vodka—the drink whose quality is linked directly to its apparent lack of qualities—has helped the Russian people to, in his words, "counter the stress of living in a less than perfect nation" (2002, 61)

As argued in the previous chapter, taking a thoroughly historical approach to the study of society means that a basic issue in need of examination is how it is that large-scale groups comprised of competing—and often contradictory—interests can generate, then reproduce, the impression of uniformity and continuity often over long periods of time and across vastly changing political and material conditions. In other words, if we all live in the midst of what the Austrian novelist, Robert Musil (1880–1942), in his novel, *The Man Without Qualities*, once called "the old storyline of the contradictions, the inconsistency, and the imperfection of life" (1996, 23), then how do we reproduce the illusion of perfection so successfully? Although it may sound flippant, for Popov a virtually invisible elixir offers at least one explanation; vodka has provided, in his words, the illusion of free choice, making possible access to a private life that is seemingly closed to the state.

I say "seemingly" for a reason, of course; as also argued in the last chapter, as scholars we ought to assume that, despite claims to the contrary among the people whose cultural products comprise our data, there is no escape from the historical (i.e., the contingent, the ad hoc) and the collective. For example, consider the fact that in the 1970s the profits from state-controlled domestic vodka sales injected 170 billion Rubles into the Soviet treasury; using conversion rates for the mid-1970s, and accounting for inflation, that is roughly equivalent to US $804 billion today.[2] This apparent sense of isolation and privacy brought about by consuming a drink with virtually no detectable qualities turns out to have been one of the financial engines that helped to make the idea of one particular collectivity possible and persuasive.

The lesson we learn from vodka is that the means by which we invent and then assert the limits of privacy are political and economic acts through and through; they are techniques for making an invariably imperfect social group seem to work by disengaging some of its participants from a storyline that makes certain forms of collective life—certain camp fires around which certain speakers get to sit—possible and others utterly unthinkable. This assists us to see claims to privacy not in some realist fashion—as a self-evident thing or state of being—but, instead, as ways of negotiating the limits of fundamentally contestable public space, making the rhetoric and techniques for establishing and monitoring the limits of the group highly effective social regulatory mechanisms. In fact, with Musil's notion of living out a storyline in mind, we can see that it is a regulatory process remarkably similar to the sort of picking, choosing, discarding, and ignoring that goes into all acts of narrative. Defined minimally as a story with a beginning, a middle, and an end, narrative structure results from the skill of ignoring countless historical moments, overlooking events, and marginalizing interactions, all in the effort to frame, exclude, enhance, isolate, and thereby raise yet others to a level of significance they could not have possessed if they were left merely as part of the continual background noise that surrounds us all. Narratives of careers, lives, and social groups therefore result from what Jonathan Z. Smith has aptly termed an economy of signification (1982, 56), whereby just some events get to count—an economy that is, as Smith argued, negotiated by means of those behaviors we call rituals that simultaneously focus and distract attention, all in the service of establishing limits in terms of which significance can be judged, thereby making comparisons, and thus meaning and identity, possible. If narrative and ritual declare significance by arranging moments that appear tactically disengaged from their inevitably competitive and imperfect context, then vodka (at least according to Popov) creates social groups by tactically disengaging people from their inevitably collective and imperfect lives by opening for them a passage of retreat into the seemingly inner, private self: the opiate of the people, indeed.

I'm hoping that, fresh from the previous chapter, readers can begin to see what all this has to do with the topic at hand: the manner in which difference, disagreement, and dissent in the homeland are routinely, and efficiently, domesticated by means of a discourse on faith. Simply put, just as vodka's apparent lack of qualities is no indication of its effects, so too there is nothing private about the rhetoric of faith.

For example, consider the January 2003 workshop my university sponsored for students on the basic beliefs and history of Islam. Prompted by the widespread interest in (and, many would no doubt hasten to add, the widespread misunderstanding of[3]) Islam that quickly became evident throughout the US soon after the September 11 attacks, the planning committee carefully considered how to structure this event. At one point early in its planning, the committee—of which I was a member, along with representatives of the local Muslim community (some of whom are professors at the University), representatives from various academic departments, and assorted student organizations on campus—considered presenting Islam in terms of its role as a social movement, or in common parlance, as a "civilization," rather than as a "religion." Made by a member of the committee who happened also to be Muslim, this suggestion (whether intentionally or not, on the part of my colleague) echoed a distinction commonly found in the current literature on Islam. A well-known representative of this position is the former Princeton University Near Eastern studies professor and the oft-cited pundit, Bernard Lewis, as in when he attempts to define Islam in the opening chapter of his recent book, *The Crisis of Islam.* "To begin with," he writes,

> the word [Islam] itself is commonly used with two related but distinct meanings, as the equivalents both of Christianity and of Christendom. In the one sense it denotes a religion, a system of belief and worship; in the other, the civilization that grew up and flourished under the aegis of that religion. (2004, 3)

Perhaps because, Lewis informs his readers, religions are concerned with matters of belief and worship (i.e., rituals that give voice to inner beliefs), and not with overt forms of political behavior, Lewis primarily concerns himself with Islam as a civilization.[4] "While generalizing about Islamic civilization may be difficult and at times in a sense dangerous," he warns his reader, "it is not impossible and may in some ways be useful" (p. 4). But since utility is a relational term—table saws are useful to carpenters but not to diamond cutters—we should ask: Useful to whom? And for what purpose?

The utility of the religion/civilization distinction was apparent in our workshop. My colleague's classificatory suggestion seemed to have been prompted by a desire not to affront the sensibilities of local, conservative Christians (a number of whom are evangelical Protestants) who, quite predictably, are represented in fairly large numbers in our part of the US. For example, not long before the initial meeting early in the autumn of 2002 to plan our workshop, the University of North Carolina at Chapel Hill had been thrust into the national headlines for, of all things, having incoming undergraduate students read Michael Sells's annotated selection of excerpts from the Qur'an (1999)—a curricular decision that was troubling enough to some North Carolina residents that a lawsuit was filed against the school by the Virginia-based Family Policy Network on behalf of three anonymous UNC students who apparently felt that the school was proselytizing. (The case was thrown out by a Federal appellate court.) Perhaps approaching our topic as the study of a "civilization," so the reasoning could have gone, might help the public to understand the event better, and thereby get something important out of it, and thereby prevent some of the problems experienced in North Carolina.

Despite this suggested classification, this was not in fact how the event was billed; instead, it was an introduction to the "religion" of Islam, with students preparing by reading chapters from the works of such standard authors on religions as Huston Smith and John Esposito, and with two scholars of religion speaking (one of whom was myself, who opened the event with a brief comment on the requirements of the publicly funded study of religion), along with an historian and a political scientist. Most interesting was that, shortly before the event, it became apparent that, despite the complete silence of the local conservative Christians, a small group of politically engaged Jewish students voiced concern regarding the possible tone of the event and whether such topics as, for example, the current Israeli/Palestinian conflict would be on the table. If so, then they requested representation at the event so that, as it was put to me by a rather impassioned young lady with whom I met along with a colleague, both sides could be represented, thus giving the attendees more "balanced" information.

Like the story of Carl upping the ante late one night in Toronto, this anecdote of a small conference on Islam in Tuscaloosa has surprising relevance for the topic at hand. Inasmuch as the mass movement once known across Europe as Mohammadism, and now as Islam, was portrayed as a religion—which is, as Lewis informed his readers, a matter of personal belief expressed in forms of private behavior we call ritual and worship—these potential critics were quite comfortable with the event, since its content would, they must have reasoned, necessarily be far removed from contemporary politics, studying instead disembodied sets of beliefs, historic origins, abstract doctrines, etc. However, inasmuch as Islam was classified as a socio-political movement, as a "civilization," this would make the event necessarily political due to its potential conflict with other civilizations—notably Israeli, or so the young lady led me to believe. At the heart of this debate over naming lies our topic: the politics of classification and the utility of the modern taxon "religion."

From the outset it was obvious to everyone on our planning committee that there was something significant at stake (for those attending the event?; for those sponsoring the event?; for those contributing to the event?), depending on how it was conceived, structured, and advertized; what was particularly interesting was that so much turned on "religion"—whether anticipating possible evangelical Christian responses or addressing pro-Israeli student concerns. But surely, it comes as no surprise that much hangs on the question of classification—what Pierre Bourdieu simply but significantly termed the struggle to have power over words (1987, 14). Classification matters; as recently observed by the US humorist, David Sedaris, recalling how his childhood neighbors, who had been away for Halloween one year, arrived at their door in costumes asking for treats a day late: "Asking for candy on Halloween was called trick-or-treating, but asking for candy on November 1st was called begging" (2003, 51). Or, consider the implications of "making a date" as opposed to "setting an appointment"—quite reasonable expectations of the sorts of physical interaction that might take place during the former would likely end up being seen by one party as actionable if the event was understood as an instance of the latter. There are clearly treats for those who master the trick of their groups' classification scheme.

Because our workshop seems to have called its object of study the right thing—a religion—unlike asking for candy on the wrong day, our public event went off without a hitch. In fact, it was quite successful; despite this Latin-based term and its modern derivations not really being at home in the context of a social movement that arose on the Arabian peninsula some 1,500 years ago, it was nonetheless a religion for us. And because it was portrayed as religion, the presenters could utilize the well-known distinction between its timeless *principles*, on the one hand, and its sadly degraded forms of subsequent *practice*, on the other—what amounts to the old essence/manifestation distinction, but applied to chronological time. In this way a specific sort of Islam was presented to the participants as normative while all others were easily relegated to the status of either aberration or degradation.

For instance, consider whether the September 11 hijackers—as suggested by the scholar of religion, Ivan Strenski—"behave[d] according to very different rules of rationality than those who are profit or power maximizing in a cost-benefit calculus of a political or economic sort" (2002, 429). On one level, this line of argumentation—which presupposes that so-called religious people operate by means of some set-apart rationality—is perfectly sensible for, as argued by the French scholar of religion, Daniel Dubuisson,

> the principles of this 'religious reason' [that scholars try to understand in their cross-cultural studies] are obvious only because they previously shaped an important part of our own intellectual instrumentation and our most intimate ways of thinking. The notions that we so willingly see as transcendental, aprioristic, or original are almost always those that are most deeply buried in our own cultural memory (2003, 198)

—which makes them particularly appealing to trot out when trying to account for anomalous behaviors. However, on another level, such explanations, when offered by scholars, leave me utterly puzzled, for I do not understand how a scholar can see any human behaviors as *not* part of a complex, historically based calculus concerning how actors understand negotiations over power and privilege (i.e., politics) to be connected to the manner in which people negotiate systems of value and exchange (i.e., economics), as well as organization (sociology), and the manner in which they authorize this series of connections by appeals to rhetorics that involve such invisible agents as gods, destiny, the market, rationality, common sense, or human nature. To my way of thinking, one need have no sympathy or affinity whatsoever for such actors' motives or actions to be able to understand that calling their actions religious and thus the result of "different rules of rationality" is merely a form of obscurantism that shelves, rather than addresses, the matters of most importance in the study of how matters of difference are negotiated and contested. Instead, why not shift the ground a bit and study this and other such conflicts in terms of how historically situated groups draw on competing sets of discursive markers to authorize their all too practical and conflicting socio-political interests? Such a shift entails seeing sacred/secular or Church/State as two ways in which some groups make it possible to plot, delineate, demarcate, and rank, all of which are some of the many ways that human beings make habitable cognitive and social worlds possible and—to their peers, at least—persuasive. As the anthropologist, Mary Douglas, phrased it in the Introduction to her influential study of classification, a basic presumption of this alternative approach is that such systems of distinction, and the punishments that attend their transgression, "have as their main function to impose system on an inherently untidy experience" (1991, 4).

Before proceeding, an important point needs to be made explicit, regarding the metaphysics of presence entailed in groups' efforts to tidy up these experiences. For example, that our Latin-based classification "religion" finds no equivalent in Arabic seems not to prevent well-meaning scholars—who otherwise lament the way some scholars trample over what they consider to be authentic, indigenous meanings that require respectful treatment—from calling Islam a religion. In fact, the Arabic term *dīn* is routinely translated as religion. But, as argued in *The Encyclopeadia of Islam*, the etymology of *dīn* involves three separate lines: (i) a Hebraeo-Arabic origin meaning "judgement" or "retribution;" (ii) an Arabic root meaning "a debt" or "money owing" that comes to mean "custom" or "usage"; and, finally (iii) a Pahlevi (i.e., Middle Persian) linguistic origin meaning "revelation" that is therefore translatable as "religion." Disagreeing with the first and third etymologies, the article's author makes a persuasive case for considering *dīn* to develop from the notion of a debt that must be settled on a specific date, which in turn leads to such successive usages as: the idea of properly following an established custom of settling debts; the act of guiding one in a prescribed direction; the act of judging whether such a prescription has in fact been followed; visiting retribution upon one who has failed to follow the required path (see Lewis *et al.* 1965, 293–96). As such, *yawm al-dīn*, or "Day of Judgement," therefore comes to signify the day when Allah gives direction to all human beings. So, much as with the relation between the geographic and prescriptive senses of such English words as "direction" and "directive," we see here a gradual conflation of social exchange and social status with geographic movement and, eventually, with rules of propriety. Accordingly, *dīn* eventually moves from the more narrow sense of a debt to be discharged to being a term that stands in for "the body of obligatory prescriptions to which one must submit" (p. 293).[5]

Therefore, it is rather misleading to suggest, as does one reference resource, that *dīn* is "*employed to mean* a religion together with its practices in general" (Glassé 1989, 99; emphasis added). Although italicizing this suggestion of intentionality may be too fine a nuance, *dīn* is not "employed to mean a religion"—as if early Arabic users were hunting for a local equivalent for what some of us now take to be the obviously universal concept that lurks deep within the word "religion"; instead, it is translated by contemporary English speakers by means of their local word, religion. What's more, if the above etymology is persuasive, then there is a great deal lost in this translation, for "the concept indicated by *dīn* does not exactly coincide with the ordinary concept of 'religion' precisely because of the semantic conception of the word" (Lewis *et al.* 1965, 293).

Just what is lost (or, keeping vodka's function in mind, we could say that from the modern State's point of view, what is gained!) is significant. For instance, consider a recent translation of the Qur'an's famous *surā* 5.3:

> Today I have perfected your system of belief
> and bestowed My favours upon you in full,
> and have chosen submission (al-Islam) as the creed for you. (Ali 1988, 98)

Or, as phrased in another popular translation of the Qur'an:

> The day I have perfected your religion for you and completed My favour to you. I have chosen Islam to be your faith. (Dawood 1983, 387)

Both "system of belief" and "creed" in the first, and "religion" and "faith" in the second, are, it turns out, English renderings of *dīn*, locking the Arabic term within a discourse on inner sentiment and individual choice concerning a series of systematically related propositions (i.e., a creed that expresses a meaning with which one either does or does not agree). Nothing could be further from the complex social, transactional basis of the concept.

But perhaps such problems with translation are to be expected, at least with N. J. Dawood's popular edition of the English language Qur'an—the first translation of the Arabic text into English idiom which, according to its publisher, has sold over one million copies since it was first published in 1956. (This sales figure alone should suffice to quiet those readers who might dismiss my use of this edition as one of the above examples, since they might see it as not being scholarly enough to take seriously.[6]) After all, in the earlier editions of his translation, "the traditional arrangement [of its chapters] has been abandoned" (1983, 11; more recent editions have reverted to the so-called traditional order of revelations), since it is aimed at the "uninitiated [i.e., Christian?] reader." Therefore, his version places the "more Biblical and poetic revelations" at the beginning and then ends with "the much longer, and often more topical, chapters" (1983, 11). Given the uproar with which some Christians greeted inclusive-language Bibles, one can only imagine how many Christians would react to a version of the Bible that had its chapters rearranged, to make it easier on novice readers.[7] Perhaps this is analogous to the understandable ways in which Jewish people respond to being told by Christians that their text is the "old testament" that has been fulfilled and thereby supplanted by one that is new and improved, or the way Canadian hockey fans greeted the digitally enhanced puck on their TV screens.

Although "[t]hese few remarks cast some light on and perhaps oversimplify the difficulties encountered in translations of the *dīn* of Kur'anic [*sic*] verses into Western languages" (Lewis *et al.* 1965, 293–94), we see that, much like the ancient Greek concept *eusebia*, or the later Latin *pietas*—terms that once signified a social value in antiquity that one was thought to possess if one properly negotiated a complex social world of differing ranks and competing entitlements—a concept of obvious public rank and social relationship (i.e., being in another's debt) has eventually come to be sentimentalized as a matter of inner faith, belief, opinion, and judgement. Because other authors have drawn attention to this process—what we might call the modernist sentimentalization of classical piety (e.g., see Smith 1998, 271)—it should suffice for me simply to present only one additional example of how historically situated relationships of contest and difference are easily minimized by means of this rhetoric of individual belief and experience. So, consider the tricks that we find in the opening pages of a recent co-written textbook, *World Religions Today* (Esposito, Fasching, and Lewis 2002). In a section of the Introduction entitled, "Understanding Religious Experience and its Expressions," the authors draw attention to the etymology of the technical term, "religion," by asking readers to picture themselves time traveling to ancient Rome and asking someone on the street: "What religion are you?" Although the spirits of some authors might be dampened after acknowledging that people in antiquity did not talk like this at all, much less speak English, they nonetheless press on with their thought experiment: "Frustrated, you try rephrasing your question and ask: 'Are you religious?' Suddenly their faces light up and they smile and say, 'Of course, isn't every-one?'" (p. 5).

time travel to ancient Rome, this exam
se to make the imaginative leap across t
(i.e., the world in which cracks happen a
d contexts inevitably clash and compet
he cracks—and artfully using various so
se choices and commitments as inevitab
d the otherwise unescapably continge
, "shit happens." Translated to the topic
equences and specific contexts, followe
creates the impression of a complete an
e fresh resin goes without notice.

lative "Washington slept here" view o
ovenance, there are no extra-discursive
ssess the authenticity and fullness of such
claim about the past can sidle up to the
spiracy theories despite one's best efforts
eed considerable shoring up if they are to
mmunities claims are authorized by sheer
zed by appeals to the age of the speaker,
terests shared by a number of speakers,
world stage, by the size of the speaker's
me scholarly pundits, legitimacy for their
atistical analysis. For instance, consider
estone bone. Leaving aside debates on
on paleographic analysis and studies of
the likelihood that the inscription refers
the box's authenticity are prompted by
on provides hard, irrefutable, empirical
other words, how does one accomplish
es of the utterly speculative "very likely"
at we find peppered throughout such
Well, given that the numbers are against
e that "[t]he names of James (Jacob),
ommon among Jews at the turn of the
artful rhetors and turn a negative into a
ur advantage. And LeMaire is up to the
mani's *A Catalogue of Jewish Ossuaries*
ossuaries bearing inscriptions, with the
een percent of the inscriptions, Jesus in
two percent. *Assuming* that each male
rs, he determines that eighteen percent
n of Joseph" would have had a brother
"over two generations, 0.05 percent

Despite this example striking me as having something remarkably in common with stereotypical paternalism of some English speakers who think that if they merely spoke loudly and slowly enough foreigners would understand them (i.e., "Are you R-E-L-I-G-I-O-U-S?"), there is something more that we can take away from this story of time travel. For, in the process of granting the inevitable historicity, contingency, and thus contestability of our terminology (i.e., demonstrating that the modern word "religion" derives from ancient Latin words, though the precise etymology is unclear; these authors favor *religare*, meaning to bind or tie something, along with the root *ligere*, meaning to act with great care or pay particularly close attention[8]), they nonetheless presuppose that the adjectival form of the modern word—which names not "something you join" but, instead, "a way of seeing, acting, and *experiencing* things" (p. 5; emphasis added)—is necessarily a universal signifier. For, in concluding that "people [in antiquity or outside the orbit of Latin-influenced modern languages and cultures] did not think of what they did as 'a religion'—a separate reality one had to choose over against another" (p. 5), the authors yet presume that the word "religion" and "religious" names some deeply human(e), interior disposition. In fact, it is not just any old disposition but, quite possibly, the most authentically human thing of all. For, as they conclude:

> Religion as a form of human experience and behavior, therefore, is not just about purely "spiritual" things. Religion is not just about gods or God. People's religiousness is as diverse as the forms of power they believe govern their destiny, whether it be the gods as forces of nature, or wealth, or political power, or the forces of history. Religious attitudes in the modern world can be discerned in what many people would consider purely secular and very "unspiritual" attitudes and behaviors in relation to power. Hence, whatever powers we believe govern our destiny will elicit a religious response from us and inspire us to wish "to tie or bind" ourselves to these powers… (Esposito, Fasching, and Lewis 2002, 7)

Apparently, everyone is religious—much as everyone apparently understands English if spoken slowly enough—whether they know it or not, and whether or not "religion" is part of their conceptual tool box.

Despite acknowledging the historicity of their terminology these authors nonetheless continue to assume that behind the changeable word there lurks an enduring, universal presence or meaning that transcends time and place. Somewhat akin to the old bait and switch used by hucksters, what they offer with one hand (i.e., attention to the historicity of our objects of study) is swiftly removed by the other (i.e., words point toward timeless concepts and meanings), and readers are left confident that behind the merely transitory appearances of their mundane, daily lives there resides an enduring permanence that is not only theirs, for it is lodged deep within the immutable confines of trans-human experience. (It is difficult not to read in this the kind of self-importance that we find both on US bumper stickers in which everyone's child is now apparently on their school's honor roll, as well as the so-called New Age penchant for recovering past lives in which everyone was undoubtedly someone far more important that they are in this life.) Unfortunately, due to their philosophically idealist presumptions, such writers do not take seriously that words *and* concepts (i.e., signifiers *and* signifieds) are both arbitrary, and thus changeable, historical artifacts; they therefore give the lie to the historian of antiquity, Peter Brown's thoughtful words: "A little history puts one firmly back in one's place." For in their case, doing only a *little history* apparently frees them significantly *from* their place! As Brown goes on to remark in his American Council of Learned Societies (ACLS) 2003 Haskins Lecture, taking history seriously

> counters the amiable tendency of learned persons to think of themselves as if they were hang-gliders, hovering silently and with Olympian ease above their field, as it has come to spread out beneath them over the years. But real life, one knows, has not been like this. We are not hang-gliders. We are in no way different from the historical figures whom we study in the distant past: we are embodied human beings caught in the unrelenting particularity of space and time. (2003, 3)

That the terrain mapped by such amiable, high-flying scholars ends up looking an awful lot like what they assumed it would look like before donning their flight suits—a point convincingly demonstrated by Berg (2000) in his study of scholarly efforts to ascertain the authenticity of *ḥadīths* (i.e., the authoritative collection of sayings attributed to the Prophet)—is not a coincidence. Such scholars would therefore be wise to consider the caution of Dubuisson, writing on the history of the classification "religion":

> Although it is fortunate that cultures mutually translate themselves and try in this fashion to understand one another somewhat better, we should not conclude that what we translate into European languages, and because we translate it without any too great difficulty, refers back to universals to which we have the key. (2003, 197)

Somewhat reminiscent of Smith who advises scholars of religion to be "relentlessly self-conscious" of their choices and analytic tools—going so far as to suggest that "this self-consciousness constitutes his primary expertise, his foremost object of study" (1982, xi)—Dubuisson concludes: "All scientific study today ought to have as its sine qua non the critical uncompromising study of its own language" (2003, 197).

Failing to heed such advice, a common-sense or folk view of a unified or authoritative historical kernel that merely reflects back to us our own interests is easy to find, both in academia and outside of it. For instance, this view was evident in a mid-April 2003 television segment on the National Broadcast Corporation's (NBC) evening news magazine show "Dateline,"

Like the previous example of
illustrates some of the tricks we u
chasm of historical happenstance
the world in which viewpoints a
By picking and choosing among
of rhetorical resins to portray the
or natural—we leave far behin
world where, to put it inelegantly
hand, the prioritizing of certain s
by ignoring just some of the gaps,
authentic narrative—so long as th

However, because the specu
history is necessarily without pr
constraints that can be used to a
narratives. Because virtually any
bar—hence the resiliency of con
to disprove them—competitors n
win the contest. While in some c
assertion, they can also be author
the gender of the speaker, the i
and, as we routinely see on the
bat (see Lincoln 1994). Among so
speculations sometimes lies in s
once again the awe-inspiring lim
its authenticity—debates that rely
the patina's distribution[13]—what i
to *the* Jesus? After all, debates on
the presumption that the inscript
evidence of theological claims.[14] Ir
the trick of adding meat to the bor
and "it seems very probable" th
scholarship (e.g., LeMaire 2002)?
us—that is, we must acknowledg
Joseph and Jesus were all fairly c
era" (2002, 33)—we had better be
positive by using the numbers to c
challenge; he begins with L. Y. Ra
(1994), which identifies 233 *know*
name of Joseph appearing in fourt
nine percent, and James/Jacob in
from this region/era had two broth
of the men named "James/Jacob so
named Jesus. He concludes that,

of the population *would likely* be called 'Jacob son of Joseph brother of Jesus'" LeMaire 2002, 33; emphasis added). *Although we have no idea if this limestone box was actually associated with the Jerusalem of antiquity* (since it is "unprovenanced"), assuming a population for Jerusalem of about 80,000 for this time period (and with fifty percent being male), he concludes that "[i]n Jerusalem during the two generations before 70 CE, there were therefore *probably* 20 people who could be called 'James/Jacob son of Joseph brother of Jesus'" (emphasis added). (LeMaire then adds a final, cautionary aside: "It is, however, *impossible* to estimate how many of these 20 people were buried in ossuaries and how many of these ossuaries would be inscribed" (emphasis added).

Despite this apparent modesty, considerable, though generally undisclosed, work is being done at the site of these compounded qualifications, work that attempts to create significance by minimizing dissension (i.e., by harnessing competing narratives of the past). This is precisely where the resin of wishful thinking—call it conservation, if you will, or maybe call it myth-making—meets the cracks of historical happenstance. For example, for LeMaire's mathematics to be persuasive one must completely overlook a whole series of gaps and fissures; we must overlook the fact that there is no necessary relationship between the number (and thereby characteristics) of inscribed ossuaries recorded in Rahmani's 1994 catalogue and some stable historical reality (e.g., the number and form of inscribed ossuaries that were actually in use in Jerusalem by 70 CE), making the numerical starting point for his calculations a banal number of no particular significance. Moreover, that there is no necessary link between the unprovenanced artifact in the ROM and life in the ancient city of Jerusalem is equally important to overlook, as is the fact that there is no necessary relation between early recorded Church tradition (coming largely from Book II of Eusebius of Caesarea's early fourth-century CE *Ecclesiastical History*) that places James's death in Jerusalem and the fact of his actual burial in Jerusalem—assuming that there was in fact an actual historical actor named James of the significance that the subsequent tradition places on him and, moreover, assuming that an artifact unearthed (bought?) in Jerusalem in the late-twentieth century indicates that the object was actually in Jerusalem in 70 CE.

With so many unacknowledged assumptions up and running, I cannot help but recall what, as a small child, I was often told happens when you *assume*; "you make an *ass* out of *u* and *me*." For only after the conservator's steady hand has done its task can we so confidently leap past the qualifications and empty spaces, as does the ROM's website when it (over)confidently concludes that "[a]lthough we cannot be certain of the identity of the people named, *the James ossuary does put us in contact with an age when there were still people alive who knew Jesus of Nazareth*" (emphasis added). However, much like Mel Gibson's Jesus, the bone box puts us in contact with no such people in no such age; recognizing that it is only by means of a discourse that the bone box becomes significant, we see that the museum's claim is akin to the manner in which the persuasiveness of urban legends is based on the fact that it always happened to a friend of a friend who saw it for herself.

Aware of these historiographical difficulties, Robert Darnton offers a wise caution that draws attention away from some stable past and refocuses it on the means whereby stable pasts are manufactured and reproduced in the present. In discussing the process whereby eighteenth-century French political rhymes and popular songs were spread, he recounts that, in the case of one particular song, he has found nine different versions in various manuscript collections. Recognizing that there is no necessary relationship between the currently existing nine and the body of popular verses that might have actually circulated in Paris throughout the mid 1700s, Darnton acknowledges something entirely alien to hang-gliding scholars such as Shanks: "It is impossible to measure the size of this corpus, but we can get some idea of its dimensions by examining all the evidence that remains in the archives" (2003a, 64). We can indeed "get some idea of its dimensions" but only by means of a contemporary discourse on the past that establishes the parameters of such things as "evidence" and "archives," all in order to delimit significance and consequence of an unruly accumulation of the stuff that we associate with people from long ago.

Apart from sheer assertion, I am not sure how one would ever provide evidence to mount a persuasive argument concerning the fact that elements of one's own conceptual framework are universal or that a limestone box is self-evidently significant; failing to recognize that one can never get outside language and conventions, many authors are playing with loaded dice, since they set up their argument by presupposing that English is a universal language, that time travel exists, or that chipped stone speaks some special language of historical significance (their version of hang-gliding). Fail to assume this and authors who attempt the trick of trying to squirm out of history have no argument. Yet, as troubling as such forms of argumentation are—if "argumentation" is even the right word—it was precisely this asserted metaphysics of enduring presence that helped to make our workshop in Tuscaloosa an uncontroversial success.

4 A Little More Authentic than was Really Necessary

As suggested earlier, there was much at stake in how we organized our one-day workshop on Islam, and that organization had something to do with a quest for timeless origins. For instance, consider how all this was phrased in a book that was suggested for the students to read:

> If the *principles of Islam* were followed, every Muslim would treat every other Muslim like a brother; in fact, they have been attacking one another almost since the founding of the faith. (Lippman 1995, ix; emphasis added)

Or, as Frederick Denny observes in the concluding lines to his introductory textbook:

> Muslims *true to their calling* should continue to invite others to the Straight Path and to hope for a day when all humans will celebrate their brother- and sisterhood in a worldwide *Umma*, reflecting God's Unity in human religious unity and harmony… (1987, 127; emphasis added)

It is obvious from the above quotations that a stable, authentic, and thus supremely normative, originary point exists, presumably communicated across the chasms of historical change through the mediation of disembodied meanings encoded within scripture and commentary, all of which—when read closely and interpreted correctly—serves as a criterion by which to judge contemporary, fractious cultural practices. In this way, one can accomplish the trick of distinguishing peaceful and authentic orthodoxy ("principles" or a "calling") from dangerous, contemporary aberrations. And just what does this essence, the principle, of Islam end up looking like? As stated clearly in the preface to Lippman's book, his aim is to distinguish the inclusivist and quietist principles of Islam conceived as a faith from the common "misconceptions and misinformation" (p. x), so as to counter the daily images we see in the US of so-called militants, guerrillas, terrorists, and extremists. And Denny's closing words clearly advocate recovering the supposed origin's unambiguous drive toward a similarly liberal, inclusive tradition that outlives all so-called parochial differences.

Despite the—to my mind, at least—convincing manner in which an author such as Michel Foucault critiqued what he referred to as the effort to write a total history—"The project of total history is one that seeks to reconstitute the overall form of a civilization, the principle—material or spiritual—of a society, the significance common to all the phenomena of a period" (Foucault 1989, 9)—we nonetheless easily find historians loathe to "abandon the elevated but somewhat unreal vantage point of the hang-glider" (to borrow once again from Peter Brown).[1] They are likely loathe to abandon them because rhetorics of tradition, and the classification of "religion" which often stands in for the symbolic heart of a tradition, are politically useful in times of social strife—which, if we presume that social groups do not move forward in time simply by means of their own momentum but, instead, continually require new investments of social capital, is pretty much always. Much as the way in which President Bush's 2004 re-election strategy involved continued reference to "September 11" as if that was a distilled or so-called "defining moment" frozen in time, as well as the way in which the presumably eternal and uniform intentions of the Founding Fathers are routinely invoked whenever a catastrophe is thought to befall the US (a point made by Darnton 2003a: x), the swift appearance in the days following the September 11 attacks of an essentialized notion of tradition—whether "our" tradition of freedom or "their" tradition of hating our freedoms—should therefore not surprise us.

Before proceeding, however, I should ensure that the focus on rhetoric and classification is not seen as merely a study in inconsequential words. For those who do not see the link between rhetoric and action (thereby perpetuating the politically useful, though intellectually troublesome, split between theory and practice, to be addressed in greater detail below), consider what is at stake in the way that, during the recent war with Iraq, the US government spokespeople and media regularly described what we might otherwise simply term "attacks" on US soldiers as "ambushes"; clearly, connotations of deceit and cowardice attach to the latter, as if one's opponents are not playing by the rules of war. Of course, it all depends on who is doing the hiding. For example, in the 1960s, comedian Bill Cosby had a wonderful stand-up routine about the US revolutionary war being fought as if it were a US football game; because the revolutionaries win the coin toss they get to decide that, while the British must wear red and march in a straight line, the revolutionaries can wear any color they wish and shoot from behind the rocks and the trees. "Ambush" or "stealth"—it all depends on who it is that's being sneaky.

Or, better yet, consider the case of the August 7–11, 2003, *Washington Post* poll in which 69 percent of the 1,003 randomly selected Americans surveyed nation-wide said that they believed that Saddam Hussein was either "very likely" or "somewhat likely" to have been "personally involved" in the September 11 attacks.[2] Despite the Bush administration finally acknowledging that it has no evidence of this (as President Bush himself acknowledged to reporters as far back as September 17, 2003[3] and as Secretary of State Colin Powell acknowledged again on January 8, 2004[4]), at the end of 2003 a joint CNN, *USA Today*, and Gallup poll found that—when asked "Do you think Saddam Hussein was personally involved in the September 11th terrorist attacks, or not?"—53 percent of the randomly selected 1,000 respondents answered "Yes, was involved."

According to the Gallup Organization's analysis of the data:

> There has been an increase in the number of Americans who feel that Hussein was personally involved in the Sept. 11 terrorist attacks, from 43% in September [2003] to 53% today [December 2003]. The level of agreement with this supposition is now similar to what it was in March of this year and in August 2002, when the question was first asked this way. The drop in September may have been a reaction to President Bush's public statement that Hussein was probably not involved in the attacks.[5]

How can one account for the fact that, just as the President admitted that "Hussein was probably not involved in the attacks," the belief yet persisted?

First off, that the latter poll was conducted just days after the widely covered December 13, 2003, capture of Saddam Hussein, must certainly be taken into account. Second, consider that as late as his December 15, 2003, year-end press conference—largely devoted to Hussein's capture—the President continued to make a number of allusions to "terrorists" in Iraq and the fact that the September 11 attack prompted the US military action in Iraq (e.g., "I will never forget the lessons of September 11, 2001" said Bush in his press conference, clearly implying a cause/effect relationship) likely plays a significant role as well.[6] Most generally, then, according to an MSNBC news story, "[t]he main reason for the endurance of the apparently groundless belief, experts in public opinion say, is a deep and enduring distrust of Hussein that makes him a likely suspect in anything related to Middle East violence."[7] Yet it is precisely this "groundless belief" that has helped to pave the way for the ground covered in the Middle East by the Coalition of the Willing.

Consumers of daytime television and newspapers therefore seem to come by this "deep and enduring distrust" honestly, insomuch as they are simply answering questionnaires based on the information that had consistently been presented to them over the preceding year. For example, consider a transcript of Vice President Dick Cheney's September 14, 2003, appearance on NBC's weekly political interview show "Meet the Press"—the appearance that prompted Bush to acknowledge, three days later, that there was in fact no evidence of a direct link. In that interview, much like the many interviews with, and speeches by, senior administration officials leading up to, as well as those given after (sometimes long after), the 2003 war with Iraq, the Vice President was careful not to claim Iraq's direct responsibility but the intimation was clear:

> Vice President Cheney: If we're successful in Iraq, if we can stand up a good representative government in Iraq, that secures the region so that it never again becomes a threat to its neighbors or to the United States, so it's not pursuing weapons of mass destruction, so that it's not a safe haven

for terrorists, now we will have struck a major blow right at the heart of the base, if you will, the geographic base of the terrorists who have had us under assault now for many years, but most especially on 9/11. They understand what's at stake here. That's one of the reasons they're putting up as much of a struggle as they have, is because they know if we succeed here, that that's going to strike a major blow at their capabilities.

Tim Russert [the host of the show]: So the resistance in Iraq is coming from those who were responsible for 9/11?

Vice President Cheney: No, I was careful not to say that.

A little later the topic of the *Washington Post* poll was raised:

Tim Russert: *The Washington Post* asked the American people about Saddam Hussein, and this is what they said: 69 percent said he was involved in the September 11 attacks. Are you surprised by that?

Vice President Cheney: No. I think it's not surprising that people make that connection.

Tim Russert: But is there a connection?

Vice President Cheney: We don't know....

Although Cheney makes no direct accusation of Iraqi involvement, a linkage has been clearly suggested. In fact, in a January 22, 2004, interview with National Public Radio's Juan Williams, Cheney went considerably further; despite Bush's and Powell's previous acknowledgements that there was no evidence of a link, he took refuge in the rhetoric of personal opinion and private belief—which will likely help if it ever comes down to claiming plausible deniability—which differs significantly from the potent rhetoric of immanent threat posed by Iraq prior to the war. "I *believe* they had programs designed to produce weapons of mass destruction.... If he [Saddam Hussein] had such a connection [to al Qaeda,] and I *believe* he did ...; there's over-whelming evidence of a connection between al Qaeda and the Iraqi government" (emphasis added)."[8]

What all this amounts to is nicely summed up by John Mueller, an Ohio State University political scientist interviewed in the earlier-cited MSNBC news story: "You get a general fuzz going around.... People know they don't like al Qaeda, they are horrified by September 11th, they know this guy [Saddam Hussein] is a bad guy, and it's not hard to put those things together.[9] So "[w]here did they get that idea?" asks Arthur Schlesinger Jr in a *New York Review of Books* essay. Answering his own rhetorical question, he adds: "Perhaps from the administration's rhetoric filtered through the press" (2003, 25).

Case in point, consider Deputy Secretary of Defense, Paul Wolfowitz's October 18, 2002, remarks. In this speech, leading up to the war, the post-war intimation of a link between Iraq and al Qaeda was far more explicit, based, Wolfowitz assured his audience, on unambiguous facts about a decade of senior-level contacts between Iraq and al Qaeda, facts about Iraqi training of al Qaeda people, including in chemical and biological weapons, and facts about Iraq providing sanctuary for al Qaeda people, including senior al Qaeda people, including in Baghdad. Combine that with the fact that the President referred to in his speech, which is not about al Qaeda but is about Iraq, that we know they're working on unmanned aerial vehicles, the capability of targeting the United States, and you begin to have facts that I think you have to make judgements against.... We're trying to lay out the facts as best we can. We're laying them out precisely and accurately. And I believe those facts more than justify the concern the President has expressed, that this regime is too dangerous to be left with the world's most dangerous weapons in its hands.[10]

Despite the "fact" that the public case for this war rested "firmly on evidence too secret to share" (as phrased by Powers 2003, 17), and the "fact" that now, long after the US has obtained virtually unimpeded access to the entire nation (despite the alarming number of US military—and, now, US civilian —deaths are still taking place on an almost daily basis in Iraq), no evidence of weapons of mass destruction (whether biological or nuclear) has been found. This is such an obvious elephant in the room for the administration that, in his January 20, 2004, State of the Union address, President Bush went so far as to refer to Iraq's pre-war threat as being comprised of "weapons of mass destruction-related program activities."[11]

Rhetoric is therefore an all-too-practical form of human activity that makes certain sorts of behaviors possible. For instance, consider the link between ways of representing/understanding reality and one's support for the war against Iraq that was made painfully apparent in a national survey conducted by the Program on International Policy Attitudes (PIPA), at the University of Maryland. Their survey was based on seven polls, of 8,634 people, and was conducted monthly between January and September 2003 (the poll was reported on October 2, 2003).[12] As reported in the press release which accompanied the poll results:

> 48% incorrectly believed that evidence of links between Iraq and al Qaeda have been found, 22% that weapons of mass destruction have been found in Iraq, and 25% that world public opinion favored the US going to war with Iraq. Overall 60% had at least one of the three misperceptions.... Among those with none of the misperceptions listed above, only 23% support the war.... [The rate rises] to 86% for those with all three misperceptions.

In fact, 20 percent reported that they believed that chemical or biological weapons *were actually used* by Iraq during the recent war. Correlating the reported news source with the respondents' perceptions, indicated that, of the respondents, 77 percent of the people who had no misperceptions consider National Public Radio (NPR) to be their "primary source of news" and 22 percent considered FOX News to be theirs. Among those who had one or more misperceptions, only 23 percent gained their news through NPR whereas 80 percent got theirs through FOX.

With all this in mind, I therefore differ with a writer such as Paul Krugman who, in reviewing two recent books on the current Bush presidency, observes that "[u]nder [George W.] Bush, it seems, political rhetoric bears no relation to reality" (2004, 6). Instead of presuming a stable reality exists, that (as Charles Taylor might have phrased it) is merely shaped by rhetoric, the position argued throughout this essay is that social rhetorics—all of which come with political implications—entrench interests for how groups assert that the world *ought* to be. Therefore, taking for granted that rhetoric is a form of political speech that makes certain social realities persuasive and thus possible—rhetorics make realities—we can turn to a specific sort of "general fuzz" that was much in the air during our workshop in Tuscaloosa, which was useful when it came to how we represented a marginal group whose members were seen to have transgressed the unarticulated rules of good form that allow entry into the so-called community of nations: the rhetoric of tradition.[13]

As argued by Foucault, the use of "tradition" bestowed what he termed a "special temporal status to a group of phenomena that are both successive and identical," enabling commentators "to rethink the dispersion of history in the form of the same," allowing them to make "a reduction of the difference proper to every beginning, in order to pursue without discontinuity the endless search for the origin" (1989, 21). Moreover, as was apparent in the work of William James, the rhetoric of tradition

> enables us to isolate the new against a background of permanence, and to transfer its merit to originality, to genius, to the decisions proper to individuals. (Foucault 1989, 21)

The rhetoric of an infinitely authoritative tradition influenced by timeless principles that are embodied in charismatic geniuses and their quoted words is therefore linked to what Theodor Adorno termed the ideology of personalization, "through which, as a clear compensation for the functionalization of reality, the value of individual people and private relationships is immeasurably overestimated in comparison to actual social determination" (2002, 196). In this way, what might instead be understood as the result of ad hoc, structural (from local to geo-political) factors—what I take Foucault to have meant by "history"—is seen as the result of the will and thus motive force of individual actors. Such personalization has specific advantages, of course, for it enables us to attribute responsibility and thus easily identifiable lines of causality, guilt, and innocence; the rhetoric of tradition and the ideology of personalization are therefore necessary if large-scale, complex, intertwined, inevitably contradictory, and profoundly self-implicating social worlds are to be provided with simplistic focal points and narrative lines that, for whatever reason, can be pitted against each other. In this way a crisis, a state of emergency, "can be manufactured through an economics that capitalizes on uncertainty by concealing it beneath the polarities of underground and above-ground, friend and foe" (Bishop and Phillips 2002, 102).

Those who benefit from this simplification and polarization "have to prevent people from paying attention," as Noam Chomsky was quoted as saying with regard to the Bush administration's official reasons for the 2003 war on Iraq, "and the only way anyone has ever figured out how to do that is to terrify them with tales of monsters who are about to destroy them" (quoted in MacFarquhar 2003a, 79). This process of making rhetorically useful monsters intent on harming innocent victims (e.g., good guy/bad guy, civilian/military, innocent/guilty) is, to draw once again on Adorno, part of "the prevalent ethos [which] is suspicious of anything which is miscellaneous, or heterogenous, of anything which has not clearly and unambiguously been assigned to its place" (2002, 190). The ideology of personalization, the technique of essentialization, the rhetorics of tradition and crisis—what one recent political commentator groups together as "junk politics" (DeMott 2003)[14]—are thus the interconnected means whereby we concoct clearly delimited places—call them the self, the nation, tradition, etc.—that seem to be uniform over time; into these places we then put the unruly stuff of our daily experience of an ambiguous world in which we live and compete with others for scarce goods—both symbolic and material.

The project of manufacturing a total, linear history therefore depends upon the unquestioned use of individualization and personification, as found most recently in George W. Bush's apparently well-received discourse of good guys versus bad guys, his jargon of "with us or against us," and his post-September 11 Wild West reference to "Wanted Dead or Alive" posters (all of which is so obviously reminiscent of the once-powerful rhetoric of Manifest Destiny as to not be worth mentioning here in any great detail, rather than just to note it). Although it is hardly surprising to find this in a politician's sound bite, it is seen also in the work of many scholarly and popular authors—on the political left as well as the right, doves as well as hawks—who, over the past decade and, most notably, following the September 11 attacks, comment on Islam as if a privileged, originary moment was its defining characteristic. As we find in virtually all tales told by members of mass movements, the inner spark is said to be carried forward throughout history by means of a homogenous tradition and those heroic representatives who embody it. In the case of American democracy, it is the Constitution and the members of the US Supreme Court who are charged with carefully reading and interpreting the text so as to determine the founding fathers' intentions.[15] In the case of classical Islam, an authoritative chain of transmitters (the *isnād*) authorize a series of stories attributed to the earliest members of the Muslim faith, the collection of which comprise tradition (*ḥadīths*). Despite tremendous rhetorical efforts used to distinguish between these two systems for determining and then communicating authenticity and thus the ongoing legitimacy of a specific conception of the group, I fail to see how the hermeneutical efforts practiced in both instances are all that different from each other.

But the pundits of the former social system—who make their regular appearances on our televisions, our radios, in our newspapers and magazines, and in our popular and academic books—are not deterred by the challenge of portraying the latter as illegitimate, even if it is based on the same sleight of hand as is their own social identity. As noted by Said in the 1997 Introduction to the revised edition of his 1981 book, *Covering Islam*:

> A corps of "experts" on the Islamic world has grown to prominence, and during a crisis they are brought out to pontificate on formulaic ideas about Islam on news programs or talk shows. There also seems to have been a strange revival of canonical, though previously discredited, Orientalist ideas about Muslim, generally non-white people. (1997, xi)

These experts work diligently to stitch together in their readers' and viewers' minds not only a homogenous view of Islam across history but, by positing "a worldwide conspiracy behind every explosion" (Said 1997, xxxiv), a homogeneity of "evil ones" that stretches across the world right now. That this presumed homogeneity flies in the face of the fact that more than one billion people, in settings as diverse as Indonesia, the former eastern Europe, not to mention North America, today identify themselves as Muslim seems not to be an issue.

The inevitable differences between such actors do not stand in the way of commentators intent on recovering the authentic core to Islam that apparently unites them all, or at least those among them who are authentically Muslim. For example, after surveying several competing, post-September 11 popular conceptions of Islam, the hawkish journalist Stephen Schwartz phrases it as follows:

> But none of these views of Islam represented an accurate accounting of its *essence*. A journey to *the authentic heart of Islam* sets one at odds with a great deal of erroneous common wisdom in the West—a situation Islamic extremists have exploited to advance their own agenda. The lack of central religious authority in Islam contributes to the problem; for outsiders it is difficult to distinguish between the margins and the mainstream. (2002, xiii; emphasis added)

With Said's just-quoted passage in mind, if the year of publication was not contained in the above citation, it would be tempting to assume that it dated from a far earlier period, perhaps the height of eighteenth- and nineteenth-century Orientalist scholarship. But Schwartz's thoughts on the extremists' agenda certainly do not date from that earlier era; instead, these "formulaic ideas" were trotted out in the wake of the September 11 attacks; the widespread nature of essentialist assumptions in the writings of contemporary political pundits from across the political spectrum suggests that Said's critique of Orientalist discourses—his sometimes homogenous view of the Occident and victimized view of the Orient notwithstanding—is as relevant now as it was when his book was first published.

Of course, the trouble with talk of ahistorical originary moments and the rhetoric of unswerving authenticity is that such talk cannot be disengaged from the speaker's expectations, interests, and agendas, all of which are solidly in the here-and-now—much like the 1960s "Star Trek" view of the future that cannot now be seen as anything but a projection of the 1960s! In fact, it is just such projected interests that allow the speaker to select this, as opposed to that, authentic, defining characteristic (on the jargon of authenticity, see primarily Adorno 1997; see also McCutcheon 2003, ch. 8). The so-called authentic characteristic rarely, if ever, goes against the speaker's interests concerning what the thing *ought* to look like—indicating that authenticity discourses are profoundly moral, political discourses in which conflicting aspects of worlds-as-they-happen-to-be are edited down and packaged as one homogenous world-as-it-ought-to-be. That the world as we find it often resists our efforts to edit it down should be obvious—but it usually isn't.

Consider the US film maker Quentin Tarantino, whose film, *Kill Bill, Volume 2* features a scene in a Mexican brothel. As described in an article on the making of the film:

> Tarantino had decided that the scene should be shot in an authentic Mexican whorehouse, so various scouts and production assistants flew to Mexico last winter and found, near an obscure beach resort ninety miles south of Puerto Valarta, the place they were looking for. When the scouts found it, the whorehouse *was more authentic than was really necessary*— it lacked a bathroom and stood across the road from a pig slaughterhouse, so the floor was covered with feces of both human and porcine origin— but the scouts got it cleaned up and sent pictures of it to the production designers in Los Angeles. (MacFarquhar 2003b, 148; emphasis added)

So, a small bar was installed by the film makers, along with a jukebox, "some tin-can lamps, a Foosball table, a few white plastic chairs, and a green parrot in a cage;" they also rented some more pigs for the slaughterhouse. Despite a subsequent murder at the whorehouse, which prompted its owner to move it a little way down the street, it was transformed into a movie set that had the look that a Mexican brothel *ought* to have—at least to the director's eyes, and, one would assume, those of US film-goers. But even after its makeover there remained a remnant of the pre-Hollywood structure—not that it is any more authentic, either!—the one that was judged "more authentic than was really necessary," for we are told that the whorehouse *qua* film set still "smelled faintly but pleasantly of dung" (MacFarquhar 2003b, 149).

It is likely not news to anyone that the finished product featured a film version of a whorehouse *qua* authentic Mexican whorehouse whose authenticity was the result of Hollywood production designers working to tame a reality that doggedly refused to fit nicely within middle-class audiences' tastes. This brings to mind the manner in which Susan Sontag (2004) makes plain how war photographers have all too often choreographed what strike the viewer as spontaneous, and thus unquestionably gritty, human, and thus authentic images of war that therefore carry with them some sort of moral authority—such as Joe Rosenthal's famous US flag raising re-enactment during World War II on the island of Iwo Jima; the staged photograph, taken by Yevgeny Fhaldei, of Russian troops raising the Russian flag above Berlin's Reichstag; or even the earlier, Crimean war photographs of Roger Fenton who rearranged cannonballs for his famous "The Valley of the Shadow of Death" photograph of the (as it turns out, mistaken) place where the infamous charge of the so-called Light Brigade took place. Reality is, as they say, a little too unruly to be authentic.[16]

Despite apparently being drawn to ennobling quests for authenticity, there sometimes occurs a negative reaction to realities that strike us as too authentic, as in when the elaborate special effects now contained in our motion pictures prevent the eye from simply taking in the entire scene and, instead, prompts us to examine in detail such things as the outline around the actor, speculating on how his figure was digitally placed into the flames of the burning house. This negative reaction brings to mind an effect termed "the uncanny valley," of which artificial intelligence designers are well aware; despite the apparently common-sense assumption that "the closer the robot resembles a human being, the more affection or feeling of familiarity it can engender" (Reichardt 1978, 26), in early studies of human responses to artificial intelligence, Japanese roboticist Masahiro Mori instead found that the strong correlation between emotional reaction (i.e., empathy) on the part of test subjects and the increasing authenticity of a robot dropped off completely when a previously unforeseen threshold of authenticity was crossed, producing what he called an "uncanny valley" (or what might also be called a trough) on the test result's graph. He found that whereas test subjects reacted increasingly positively to such things as a stuffed toy, an industrial robot, and a human-shaped robot, they reacted negatively to such things as a prosthetic hand, handicapped people, a Bunraku puppet (a traditional form of Japanese puppetry using approximately half life-sized puppets), and an ill person. Mori's findings—which, most recently, have been cited in media attempts to explain why Gollum, the computer-animated character who figured prominently in *The Lord of the Rings* films, would more than likely *not* be nominated for such things as an Academy Award—indicated that, in order for a positive response on the part of humans, a prosthesis or a robot should always bear obvious marks of its construction. In fact, this may help to account for the popularity of overtly violent films such as Tarantino's, given that his work presents obvious caricatures of explicit violence.[17]

The opposite problem—something being a little too *inauthentic* for its own good—has recently come to light: consider the case of the Andy Warhol Authentication Board (formed eight years after the artist's death in 1987) and its recent decisions against authenticating prints that previously were understood by their owners to be authentic—and thus extremely valuable—Warhols (Shnayerson 2003). That Warhol became famous for his mass-produced pop art—think of his Campbell's soup can prints or the garishly colored prints of Marilyn Monroe and Jackie Kennedy (all of which have sold for millions of dollars)—makes this recent controversy all the more interesting. In fact, in *The Sunday Telegraph* article that reported on this controversy,[18] it was noted that even a Polaroid taken by the artist can be valued as high as £12,000 (yet in the early 1990s they were going for a mere $1.00 each)! But just what constitutes an authentic Warhol (much as determining which version of de Chirico's "The Disquieting Muses" is the "original" original) is no easy task. For, as John Paul Russell, Warhol's printer throughout the 1980s, is quoted in the *Telegraph*: "I had never seen Andy Warhol even once come down to the studio in Tribeca [in New York City] to watch his work being printed."

The problem turns out to be the very thing that seems to have made Warhol stand out in the history of pop art in the first place; as phrased by the *Telegraph* art correspondent:

> The serious problem facing the authentication board … is that Warhol, having come up with the concept for a work, often delegated the manual labour to other people—thereby making it difficult to ascertain who "made" the piece.

Much like Tarantino's production designers hot on the scent of a Mexican brothel, in attempting to determine the provenance of the works the authentication board seems to have no recourse but to divine the "intent" of the artist. But this is no easy task. "When the board declares works 'not the work of Andy Warhol,' does it just mean actual fakes?" asks Michael Shnayerson in his *Vanity Fair* article on the controversy. "Or does it … often mean works that were by Warhol, but not in the board's opinion *intended* by the artist to be shown or sold as art?" (2003, 201; emphasis added). Although one might hope that the determination of authorial intent is more reliable than reading one's future in, say, tea leaves or entrails, a generation of critical literary theorists has concluded that, as with judging claims about the past, one can literally only imagine the criterion to establish its reliability; change the interests, and the imagination along with its criteria change as well. Predictably, then, some have argued that the Board is seeking to manipulate the worldwide Warhol market by controlling what gets to count as a Warhol work (none other than playing the old economic game of limiting supply to increase demand and thus value). Whatever the reason, many of Warhol's assembly-line-produced copies, reportedly signed or even given by him directly to some of the people who now find that they no longer own a real Warhol, are just a little too fake to be chic. "It's in trying to draw this line, between art and non-art, that the Warhol authentication board seems to get hopelessly—absurdly—bollixed up" (Shnayerson 2003, 216).

To some it might be news that representations seemingly far removed from the reach of the movie production designer and pop artist's factory are just as liable to be tinkered with by those designers and artists that go by the names of experts, journalists, editorialists, politicians, and, not least of which, scholars. As observed by Slavoj Žižek, these cultural engineers had direct access to an understandably confused public after the attacks on the World Trade Center and the Pentagon.

> In the days after September 11, the media reported that not only English translations of the Koran but also books about Islam and Arab culture in general became instant bestsellers: people wanted to understand what Islam is, and it is safe to surmise that the vast majority of those who wanted to understand Islam were not anti-Arab racists, but people eager to give Islam a chance, to get a feel for it, to experience it from the inside, and thus to redeem it—their desire was to convince themselves that Islam is a great spiritual force which cannot be blamed for the terrorist crimes. (2002, 34)[19]

Despite the, no doubt, good intentions of the reading public to learn something about the world around them, the attempts of such pundits to get inside authentic Islam are no less "bollixed up" than efforts to establish a clear distinction between, say, friend and foe or, as became apparent in the UN debates that followed in the wake of September 11, between freedom fighter and terrorist.[20] Taking these conundrums for granted, it falls to the culture critic to sniff out the faint waft of dung which inevitably hangs in the air when we attempt to sanitize the unsightly and the unruly by means of binary distinctions portrayed as natural. For it is the faint odor of rhetorical bullshit that provides evidence that the world of cultural artifacts is infinitely more complex than the representations of those who pit naïve innocents against the coldly calculating guilty would have us think.

A striking, and surprisingly explicit, example of the rhetorics of tradition and authenticity used to produce a specific sort of palatable (palatable *to whom* is the question in need of asking!) Islamic mainstream for US readers can be found in a *New York Times* opinion/editorial piece written by the noted British novelist, Salman Rushdie, not long after the September 11 attacks. After detailing how "radical politics" had co-opted "a faith"—what he terms "the obscurantist hijacking of their religion"—he concludes his article by writing:

> Many of them [those Muslims who currently advocate the need for what Rushdie significantly terms a "Reformation in the Muslim world"] speak of another Islam, their personal, private faith.
> The restoration of religion to the sphere of the personal, its depoliticization, is the nettle that all Muslim societies must grasp in order to become modern.... If terrorism is to be defeated, the world of Islam must take on board the secularist-humanist principles on which the modern is based, and without which Muslim countries' freedom will remain a distant dream. (2001, A25)[21]

Given Rushdie's own history with so-called Islamic extremism, it is perhaps understandable that he recommends this Protestant-styled interiorization. As phrased by the well-known pundit, John Esposito, the question to which writers such as Rushdie are offering an answer is: "Have they [i.e., the "religious extremists"] hijacked Islam for their own unholy purposes, or do they, as they claim, represent a return to the authentic teachings of the faith?" (2003, x). Given the subtitle of his latest book—*Terror in the Name of Islam*—it is more than obvious that Esposito agrees with Rushdie in recovering an apolitical authenticity: Islam, Esposito asserts, "like Judaism and Christianity, rejects terrorism" (p. ix). He argues that we therefore need to distinguish "between a religious or ideological alternative or challenge and a direct political threat," which in turn prompts him to recommend that we distinguish "between the *unity of Islam* and the diversity of its *multiple and complex manifestations* in the world today, between the violent actions of the few and the legitimate aspirations and policies of the many" (Esposito 1999, 3; emphasis added).

A useful example of this sort of argument—an example that makes evident that things are not as clear cut as such writers portray them as being—can be found in Vincent Cornell's previously quoted contribution to *Dissent from the Homeland: Essays after September 11*. After citing three hadiths that counter contemporary views concerning the glory (i.e., young virgins, etc.) supposedly awaiting those who seek martyrdom (e.g., Palestinian suicide bombers), Cornell asks rhetorically whether "this is enough to convince readers that extremists have hijacked 'true' Islam?" Answering his own question, he adds: "Most non-Muslims would probably hope so. But the people for whom these teachings are intended would probably not listen to them. The ideologues of fundamentalism are well aware that the nature of one's religion depends on the scriptures one reads" (2003, 86).

So, in the example of Cornell we have, on the one hand, a scholar conversant with social theory and who understands all mass movements to be changeable historical processes, something evident when, a few pages later, we read: "The concept of authenticity helps maintain cultural control" (2003, 89). Yet what does one make of the cultural control made possible by his use of "ideologues," his confidence in what ought to be understood as "basic Islamic doctrines" overlooked by extremists and their unwitting apologists (p. 91), let alone his repeated use of hadiths—whose authority is premised not only on the presumed authenticity of an original saying of the Prophet but on the assumption of an uninterrupted and homogenous tradition of transmission—to support his argument concerning what ought to count as normative (dare I say, authentic) Islam?

For instance, after observing that "Sufis have long maintained that the corruption of the religious scholar and the distortion of religious knowledge are the most profound and difficult moral tests that Islamic society must undergo," Cornell adds:

> The Prophet Muhammad was aware of this problem. He was aware of how the interpretation of religion depends on human perceptions. The Prophet related that God said, "I am whatever My servant thinks of Me." What do we American Muslims know of God today, when in our mosques and Islamic centers we talk more about politics than spirituality? (2003, 86–87)

As with those who read the work of the influential historian of religions, Mircea Eliade, and have difficulty distinguishing his descriptions of people's normative claims from his own normative, ontological claims, after first reading the above passage I was left wondering whether Cornell believes that hadiths are inherently authoritative or whether he cites the hadith simply as an example of how competing notions of Islam exist, all of which illustrate his point that "the nature of one's [sic] religion depends on the scriptures one reads." Does a hadith tell us what an historical agent named Muhammad knew and thought or does it inform us about an all too contemporary discourse on Muhammad? Any confusion is cleared up, however, when we read Cornell's thoughts on the "most important principles" of Islam and the manner in which "self-immolation for the wrong reason" (which suggests that there are right reasons?) "is a serious perversion of faith" (2003, 91). Apparently, there is a uniform, authentic Islam; it's just that it isn't the one of the so-called ideologues.

Despite his best scholarly intentions, then, Cornell seems to have little choice but to play the same authenticity card in developing his response to the so-called extremists that they themselves play in authorizing their sense of the direction in which this mass movement ought to be going: both rely on an ahistorical view of the past as a linear and uniform medium in which pristine meanings are communicated from an originary moment to the present. Apart from championing a version of Islam far more at home in a US setting—"an Islamic worldview that embraces diversity, equality of the sexes, and the freedom, not only to be right, but also to be wrong" (2003, 93)—Cornell's use of hadiths to authorize but one type of Islam is evidence that, no less than those he criticizes for their use of the past, his work is but one more example of (to borrow his own words) "romantic discourses of traditionalism that seek to build Islamic civilization on idealized models of the past" (p. 94). Whether politically left, middle, or right, "Islamic [or, for that matter, any other sort of] romanticism perpetuates the myth of static traditionalism" (p. 94).

We can take Karen Armstrong to represent this view when—as stated in the closing lines of her no doubt widely-read, one-page *Time* magazine essay entitled, "The True, Peaceful Face of Islam," that appeared within weeks of the September 11 attacks—she writes:

> The vast majority of Muslims, who are horrified by the atrocity of Sept. 11, must reclaim their faith from those who have so violently hijacked it. (2001, 48)

Or, as the same point was made by British Prime Minister, Tony Blair, in an October 4, 2001, speech to Parliament: "this atrocity appalled decent Muslims everywhere and is wholly contrary to the true teaching of Islam."[22] As he said in a statement three days later:

> I wish to say finally, as I've said many times before, that this is not a war with Islam. It angers me, as it angers the vast majority of Muslims, to hear bin Laden and his associates described as Islamic terrorists. They are terrorists pure and simple. Islam is a peaceful and tolerant religion and the acts of these people are wholly contrary to the teachings of the Koran.[23]

As he elaborated soon after (October 19, 2001), as part of a press conference with Arab journalists:

> I do not believe that those that committed the acts of 11 September represent in any shape or form the true faith of Islam, or the true spirit of the teaching of the Koran. And far more important than my saying that, I think that sentiment has been echoed by Muslims the world over, by clerics and scholars of Islam, and by the vast majority of people in the Arab world too.[24]

The same point was part of President Bush's September 17, 2001, comments on the occasion of a visit to the Islamic Center of Washington, DC:

> These acts of violence against innocents violate the fundamental tenets of the Islamic faith. And it's important for my fellow Americans to understand that. The English translation is not as eloquent as the original Arabic, but let me quote from the Koran itself: In the long run, evil in the extreme will be the end of those who do evil. For that they rejected the signs of Allah and held them up to ridicule. The face of terror is not the true faith of Islam. That's not what Islam is all about. Islam is peace. These terrorists don't represent peace. They represent evil and war.[25]

And in his September 20, 2001, televised address to a joint session of the US Congress, he noted that "[t]he terrorists practice a fringe form of Islamic extremism that has been rejected by Muslim scholars and the vast majority of Muslim clerics—a fringe movement that perverts the peaceful teachings of Islam."[26]

Whether or not such writers as Rushdie, Esposito, Armstrong, along with Blair's and Bush's speech writers, are correct in their nostalgic portrait of an Islamic faith or their apparent understanding of freedom as a seemingly abstract and stable Platonic form that threatens so-called fundamentalists, along with Schwartz they understand that the price of admission to the camp fire we call modernity (i.e., free-market capitalism combined with liberal democracy as found in some modern nation-states) is, at least in part, made possible by the sort of privatizations that we saw long ago in Martin Luther's *sola scriptura* and John Wesley's "strange warming of the heart," and which today is firmly entrenched in the well-established liberal tradition of distinguishing the relatively apolitical freedom "to believe" from the obviously political freedom to behave, organize, and oppose. It is none other than the rhetorical distinction between private and public—so effectively used during what we today call the Protestant Reformation—that makes possible both the internalization of dissent and the conformity of practice.[27] In fact, without this interiorization, which Schwartz associates with the Muslim commitment to mercy and compassion, there would be no way for such polemicists to advocate a "faith-based initiative for peace" in the Middle East in contradistinction to such an incendiary term as Schwartz's "Islamofascism" (p. xxii).

The handy folk assumption that drives such polemics utilizes the rhetoric of tradition, fueling the view that those features of human society we commonly call religion (as a form of experience) are somehow set apart from the natural world of derivative, historical happenstance, as William James might have said; religions are thus concerned with some posited inner goodness, enduring deep emotion, private aesthetic experience, first revealed in their originary moments—what Rushdie depoliticized as the "sphere of the personal"—thus precluding actions that either contribute to or challenge the contemporary *status quo*. It is an understanding found whenever religion is discussed, either in the academy or on Main Street, but which is particularly useful when it comes to representing marginal or dissenting movements in a manner conducive to the practical interests of dominant groups.

For instance, consider the following quotation, taken from the preface to Armstrong's best-selling *Islam: A Short History*, which occupied a prominent place in those post-September 11 book displays observed by Žižek.

> The *external history of a religious tradition* often seems divorced from *the raison d'être of a faith*. The spiritual quest is an *interior journey*; it is a psychic rather than a political drama. It is preoccupied with liturgy, doctrine, contemplative disciplines and an exploration of the heart, not with the clash of current events. Religions certainly have a life outside the

soul. Their leaders have to contend with the state and affairs of the world, and often relish doing so.... But all this is generally seen as an abuse of a sacred ideal. These power struggles are not what religion is really about, but an unworthy distraction from the *life of the spirit*, which is conducted far from the madding crowd, unseen, silent, and unobstructive. (2000, ix; emphasis added)

Or, doing what she no doubt understood to be well-intentioned and much-needed damage-control journalism in *Time* magazine, she phrased the same point as follows:

during the 20th century, the *militant form of piety* often known as funda-mentalism erupted in every major religion as a rebellion against modernity.... Fighting, as they imagine, a battle for survival, fundamentalists often feel justified in ignoring the more compassionate *principles of their faith*. But in amplifying the more aggressive passages that exist in our scriptures, they distort the tradition.

It would be as grave a mistake to see Osama bin Laden as an *authentic representative* of Islam as to consider James Kopp, the alleged killer of an abortion provider in Buffalo, N.Y., a typical Christian or Baruch Goldstein, who shot [and killed] 29 worshipers in the Hebron mosque in 1994 and died in the attack, a true martyr of Israel. (2001, 48; emphasis added)[28]

It would appear, then, that a position is allowed to count as religious, true, pious, and authentic if, *and only if*, it is politically ineffectual and reserved only for some posited interior, personal struggle of faith. Otherwise, it is classified as militant piety and cast off as part of the secondary and thus derivative history of mere changeable appearances. It is just this assumption that enables such commentators to reduce "Islam" to, in the words of Said, "a small number of unchanging characteristics despite the appearance of contradictions and experiences of variety that seem on the surface to be as plentiful as those of the West" (1997, 11).

It is to harness just these contradictions—as with the names we give to all mass movements, "Islam" is routinely used by a variety of actors to authorize all sorts of actions across a bewilderingly wide spectrum—that the rhetoric of tradition and faith are used. But "[t]he most ironic thing of all," Said notes elsewhere, is that, regardless of their position along the political divide and regardless of the particular set of so-called sacred ideals that they end up calling Islam, there is complete agreement on the part of those who employ such essentialist rhetorics "that what they are discussing is the single object they both call Islam" (2002, 70). That all of these so-called essential Islams end up looking rather different from each other, despite each being authorized in much the same fashion, suggests that the means whereby authenticity is asserted smells faintly but pleasantly of dung.

5 Another Reason Why Societies Need Dissent

Keeping in mind the now common truism that religion is a purely personal experience and that sacred ideals are, by strictest definition, politically ineffectual spiritual quests, peaceful religion's antithesis arises when this disembodied faith is found "entering the political realm" (as this grave transgression is phrased by Pinto [1999: 1]); this is an intolerable sin and a theoretical problem to be closely scrutinized by scholars all along the political spectrum. The problematic that occupies writers such as Charles Kimball and Jessica Stern is that oppositional or marginal group members (whomever "they" happen to be) sometimes "dare to *take their beliefs seriously*," as Slavoj Žižek has most recently phrased it (2003, 7). Or, as phrased by Susan Sontag, only as a result of material affluence has what was once called "news" been converted into "entertainment," and "participants" been able to conceive of themselves as "spectators." Such affluence provides groups with what Sontag refers to as "the luxury of patronizing reality" (2003, 110–11)—or what I would refer to as the luxury of patronizing competing senses of reality—enabling members of dominant groups to act "as if" they no longer believe. They can thereby displace belief onto the proverbial "Other," as Žižek argues, allowing deep, seemingly irrational belief to be smuggled back into their own worlds vicariously, by means of the back door.[1]

As he goes on to write:

> Today, we ultimately perceive as a threat to culture those who live their culture immediately, those who lack a distance toward it. Recall our outrage when, two years ago, the Taliban forces in Afghanistan destroyed the ancient Buddhist statues at Bamiyan: although none of us enlightened Westerners believe in the divinity of the Buddha, we were outraged because the Taliban Muslims did not show appropriate respect for the "cultural heritage" of their own country and the entire world. Instead of believing through the other, like all people of culture, they really believed in their own religion, and thus had no great sensitivity toward the cultural value of the monuments of other religions—to them, the Buddha statues were just fake idols, not "cultural treasures." (Žižek 2003, 7)[2]

Unfortunately, or so it is argued by members of luxurious groups, militant dissenters do not play by "civil," "rational," or "reasonable" rules; as this view is phrased by Cass Sunstein, in his recent book, *Why Societies Need Dissent*. "I do not suggest that dissent is always helpful," he writes. "Certainly we do not need to encourage would-be dissenters who are speaking nonsense" (2003, 7). Despite the familiar argument that dissenting voices (much like a free press) benefit society by helping to keep unregulated the supposedly free flow of new ideas thought to be essential in liberal democracies, it is somehow apparent to writers such as Sunstein that some dissent is just plain old nonsense and some new ideas are utterly unreasonable. The free flow of ideas is apparently not as free as one might think.

As Žižek puts it, dissenters who are dismissed in this manner apparently do not share the dominant groups' luxurious sense of irony and, at least according to some commentators, live too immediately in the present, their beliefs too linked to their actions, thus lacking our reasonable detachment. For instance, regardless how often seemingly neutral and objective commentators remind their readers of such things as that the *original*, and therefore presumably the correct, meaning of *jihād* is merely "spiritual striving" or "inward struggle" (predictably, Armstrong makes this very case [2001, 48], committing the old genealogical fallacy), there are yet other polemicists, with obviously different motives, who have no trouble extending the term's semantic range far beyond the confines of the private self. To combat the semantic ambiguity of such terms, we continue to hang on to the normative understanding that "[d]isciplined reform is called in Islam *jihād*, or striving in the ways of God.… It has found political and military expression over the centuries, but the greatest *jihād* is for every person to strive against his or her own carnal soul" (Ayoub 1996, 386).[3] Yet those without our sense of distance and irony have the audacity to "see in Islam as much a political ideology as a religion" (Roy 1994, vii), thereby putting their different beliefs into practice—a practice that, according to some, unjustifiably extends practice and commitment beyond the walls of voluntary associations where practices can be classified as rituals of merely symbolic significance.

If citing so-called popular authors—or, say, citing a best-selling world religions textbook author, such as Huston Smith, who, despite assuring his readers that Islam is not monolithic (2001, 75), nonetheless worries over "how to realize the unity that is latent in Islam when the forces of nationalism work powerfully against it" (p. 92)[4]—does not suffice to make the point being argued throughout, then consider a recent two-part review essay, by the respected US anthropologist Clifford Geertz (2003a and 2003b), in which he examines a number of recent books on Islam. "[W]e are in this country right now," Geertz accurately observes,

> engaged in the process of constructing, rather hurriedly, as though we had better quickly get on with it after years of neglect, a standard public-square image of "Islam." (2003a, 27)

But—as he goes on to say in the opening lines of the second part of his review—because the settled concepts by means of which Americans apparently once understood the world have, "since the end of the cold war," collapsed, we are left to find our way through vast collections of strange and inconsonant particulars without much in the way of assistance from finely drawn, culturally ratified natural kinds. (2003b, 36)

But this is not quite right; despite his own early work, in which Geertz, like Huston Smith cited above, advised against presuming any easy approach to understanding Islam as a monolith (Geertz 1968), soon after suggesting that in this brave, new world we have no choice but to come up with new ways of understanding the Other, in his 2003 essays he goes down the well-trod path of distinguishing internal faith—which is, by definition, non-threatening to the *status quo*—from all forms of public, political action that overtly threatens the *status quo*. To quote Said, commenting on the work of the most influential French Orientalist of the early twentieth century, Louis Massignon (1883–1962), but equally applicable to Geertz as well, it seems that "no scholar … can resist the pressures on him of his nation or of the scholarly tradition in which he works" (1979, 271). Evidence of the tremendous appeal of these techniques is provided by Geertz's own words:

> More than any other single thing it has been the rising tendency to *ideologize faith* in so much of the Muslim world that has made it increasingly hard to arrive at summary accounts of what is happening there. The movement from religion to religious-mindedness, from Islam to Islamism, from a rather quietist, withdrawn, and scholastic immersion in the fine details of law and worship, the ordinary piety of everyday life, to an activist, reformist, increasingly determined struggle to capture secular power and turn it to spiritual ends, has transformed what once was, or seemed to be, a historical macro-entity to be set beside Christianity, the West, science, or modernity, into a disorderly field of entangled differences about which it is difficult to say anything at all except that it seems at once various and volatile. (2003b, 36; emphasis added)

Much could be made of Geertz's use of "piety" in this quotation; for it is now widely used synonymously with "religion" to signify an inner, spiritual sentiment. As previously mentioned, it is fruitful to compare this to its far earlier, classical Greco-Roman use when it signified a quality that resulted from having successfully steered the course through a hierarchical social world (from gods to slaves) of varying public obligations, duties, and deference. "Ordinary piety" today, therefore, means something entirely different from what it once might have meant. As argued by Jonathan Z. Smith (1998), the gradual sentimentalization of *pietas* is but another instance of the politically efficacious discourse on faith—something also seen in the transition of Christian conceptions of the Devil from the Middle Age's notion of a malevolent external threat to the modern notion of evil as a quality of human nature, the "demon within" (Mushembled 2004). With this in mind, we see the sort of political work being done in Geertz's apparent longing for a time when Islam was simply either the scholastic penchant for debating the minutiae of law, on the one hand, or the heart-felt prayers of so-called ordinary piety, on the other—what I take to mean scholarly and domestic (hence private) Islam, in contradistinction to what Armstrong termed its "external history," that which is now widely known as "political Islam" found in so-called Islamist movements scattered throughout the world.

Although it may be obvious, the now common term "political Islam" presupposes its antithesis, non-political (or religious, spiritual, faithful) Islam. So, whereas a Muslim is religious and thus apolitical—and thereby a compliant token of difference easily tolerated—an Islamist is political and thus fanatical, deserving no toleration whatsoever. To help make this point, consider definitions for some of these terms offered by the experts. According to Graham Fuller, writing in his recent book, *The Future of Political Islam*,

> I employ the broad definition of an Islamist to denote anyone who believes that Islam has something important to say about how political and social life should be constituted and who attempts to implement that interpretation in someway. (2003, 47)

Or, in the words of Najib Ghadbian, the term Islamist refers to:

> All individuals and groups seeking to change their societies by deriving their ideology from Islam. While these groups and individuals differ in methods, approaches, styles, and substantive issues, they agree on the positive worth of Islam and the relevance of its basic concepts and values to the contemporary world. They want to shift the frame of reference in the public realm to one in which Islam, in its varying interpretations, is a major shaping force. (1997, 59)

The use of the term "political Islam" seems, at least in part, inspired by the troubles such authors see with assuming that the Protestant-derived term "fundamentalism" is a sufficient way to name these groups. The reasons offered by Beinin and Stork for dropping "fundamentalism" are: the model of Biblical literalism associated with Protestant fundamentalism is not sufficiently applicable to the long history of Islamic scholarship on the interpretation of the Qur'an; the fundamentalist aim to restore "a pure, unsullied, and authentic form of the religion, cleansed of its historical accretions, distortions, and modernist deviations" is not accurate since such so-called Islamists are actually seeking to "revitalize and re-Islamize modern Muslims societies" (Beinin and Stork 1997, 3; see also Esposito 1999, 5–6 for his related reasons for preferring "Islamic revivalism" or "Islamic activism" over "Islamic fundamentalism"). Yet, ironically perhaps, following Beinin and Stork's second understanding of fundamentalism, the "authentic faith vs. degraded practice" distinction employed by so many politically liberal commentators when addressing Islam in the post-September 11 context may itself be a wonderful example of fundamentalist rhetoric—just that it is being used by us! For fundamentalism could simply be defined as a social rhetoric that "involves a return to cultural roots in order to reform the present against the aberrations of the immediate past" (Turner 2002, 113). If so, then this suggests that there is more to the "clash of rival fundamentalisms" thesis than might at first be apparent, for on both sides of these political clashes there is a nostalgia that has become the "idiom of cultural complaint ... defined as a yearning for the past in response to a loss, absence or discontinuity felt in the present" (Grainge 1999, 631; on the politics of this nostalgia in the study of religion, see McCutcheon 1997; on rival fundamentalisms, see Ali 2002; R. Johnson 2002, 212).

The problems with such labels as militant piety or political Islam is, of course, that an obviously normative politics drives their use. Accordingly, Bruce Lawrence's warning concerning the ways in which "fundamentalism" were once used provides a sober caution for all efforts to identify and thus name so-called fanatical movements, for such terms imply

> the usurpation of political authority by militant religious ideologues. It implies a process of destabilizing the "true" leaders of the Muslim world, leaders who are deemed to be "true" because they are moderate, which is to say, West-oriented. It implies replacing "true" leaders with atavistic clones of Saladin or Genghis Khan. (1989, 190)

Failing to heed such a caution, the editors to a collection of essays also bearing the title, *Political Islam*, phrase it as follows:

> We term the movements examined in this volume "political Islam" because we regard their core concerns as temporal and political. They use the Qur'an, the *hadiths*..., and other canonical religious texts to justify their stances and actions. And they do so in all sincerity. (Beinin and Stork 1997, 3–4)[5]

"Political Islam" and "Islamist," then, are the overly generous (i.e., vague and of little analytic utility) labels given to—and I paraphrase only slightly—virtually anyone who (i) believes that the mass movement known as Islam has anything whatsoever to do with contemporary life and (ii) puts this belief into practice in some fashion. (With such a wide definition in mind, at least Fuller acknowledges—somewhat under-statedly—that "Islamists vary politically across a wide spectrum.") Members of so-called politicized religious movements are therefore those who, according to these commentators, *mistakenly* think that their beliefs have something to do with their behaviors, the behaviors of others, and the institutions in which they live and interact. While I would argue that all beliefs are intimately intertwined with behaviors (going so far as to suggest that belief is part of a discourse, thus making it a type of social behavior—but more on this below), the explicit link between beliefs and behaviors (i.e., praxis) requires an apology *only* in the case of marginal social groups that offer a political vision that is thought to be in competition with that of the so-called West. Only members of dominant social formations have the luxury of taking for granted that their beliefs and behaviors are, as Emile Durkheim once described it in his famous definition of religion, part of "un systéme solidare." One needs to look no further than an author cited earlier, Vincent Cornell, or perhaps even better, Irshad Manji, whose book, *The Trouble with Islam: A Muslim's Call for Reform in Her Faith* (2003), advocates an openly liberal political program akin to Cornell's, both of which are justified through appeals to Muslim tradition.[6] Yet these forms of obviously Islamic praxis are more than likely legitimate in the eyes of the commentators cited above because of the manner in which authors such as Cornell and Manji use Islamic theology to extend and thus normalize preferences that are seen here at home as self-evident. For example, despite the widely recognized dangers of political Islam, Manji's book has been heralded (at least according to the jacket blurbs) as "tightly reasoned," "wonderfully written," and "blazingly articulate"—perhaps because the picture of emigrant Islam that results has much in common with the pictures painted by such writers as Bernard Lewis and Karen Armstrong, both of whom are prominent among Manji's sources.

As is perhaps evident from various commentators' use of such terms as "ideology" and "ideologue," Clifford Geertz's use of the normative phrase "ideologize faith" pretty much sums up the logic that drives the use of "political Islam" and "Islamist": authentic faith is private and apolitical whereas false or politically-charged faith (i.e., ideological in either sense of the term) is a grave misuse and an inauthentic expression. Despite his chastising of Armstrong for what he terms her "just-so Sunday-school tale too simplistic to be credible, too coherent to convince, too deeply absorbed in its inner impulses" (2003a, 29–30), Geertz's own Orientalist nostalgia for an apolitical and esoteric Islamic "faith" is not only just as simplistic but equally polemical because it is just as deeply implicated in the presumption of inner impulses and unseen essences that are so handy in managing populations comprised of competing interests. Therefore, this is not an error in his interpretation so much as a crucial rhetorical feature of his work, a feature that enables authors like him to make convincing normative judgements regarding which of the many Islams is to be granted the status of authentic and thus which adherents are to be celebrated as peaceful and tolerant (apparently, those who are Muslim only in their own heads or behind the closed doors of their mosques), and which end up being seen as having no provenance. The former get to count as citizens, business partners, and allies whereas the latter are termed fanatics and imprisoned as unlawful combatants or hunted as terrorists.

Before readers misunderstand my point, let me draw attention to the manner in which this politically efficacious rhetoric of interiority functions for yet another US writer, this time one rather different from such authors as Armstrong and Geertz, yet one doing much the same socially formative work with it. Consider, for example, Malcolm X's famous "The Ballot or the Bullet" speech, delivered in April 1964. Near the start of the speech he observed that

> Islam is my religion, but I believe my religion is my personal business; it governs my personal life, my personal morals, and my religious philosophy is personal, between me and the god in whom I believe. ... Were we to come out here discussing religion we'd have too many differences from the outside and we could never get together. So today, though Islam is my religious philosophy, my political, economic, and social philosophy is black nationalism. As I say, if we bring up religion, we'll have differences, we'll have arguments, we'll never be able to get together. But if we keep our religion at home, keep our religion in the closet, keep our religion between ourselves and our god, then when we come out here we'll have a fight that's common to all of us against an enemy who is common to all of us.[7]

We see here the use of the same rhetoric of privacy aligned with the religion/politics distinction, all of which functions to suppress what the speaker likely understood as potentially irreconcilable differences, all for the sake of what he understood to be an emergent coalition that could manage collective action focused on newly shared goals. Recall that this era marks the early phase of the development of what we today refer to as black nationalism and that this speech was delivered in various locales in the north, to audiences not necessarily comprised of black Muslims. Malcolm X's rhetoric of private faith versus public action was therefore used to bring about a particular kind of group identity by providing his audience's diverse membership with the means by which to internalize the potentially conflicting social interests and differing allegiances that they brought with them to the meeting that evening.

This piece of rhetoric comprises an ideal case study in the manipulation of what Bruce Lincoln has termed social sentiments. These sentiments are

> ambivalent mixes in which potential sources of affinity are (partially and perhaps temporarily) overlooked or suppressed in the interests of establishing a clear social border or, conversely, potential sources of estrangement are similarly treated in order to effect or preserve a desired level of social integration and solidarity. (1989, 10)

Surely an accurate description of this process will make use of the private/public distinction, thus reproducing the notion that internal, religious belief is apolitical and concerned with deep issues of feeling and morality, whereas organized public action is political through and through. But if the premise that makes the human sciences possible is that human behaviors *always* begin from, and endlessly refer to, messy historical and thus public entanglements, then to study the speech's effects requires one to redescribe it as a handy piece of rhetoric working to construct a novel coalition by submerging and internalizing possible disagreement for the sake of new forms of collective action.

With Lincoln's notion of suppression in mind, there may be no better way to phrase it than to say that the categories "private," "faith," and "religion" here function repressively inasmuch as they name that which—for the sake of some imagined group's future well-being—*cannot be acted upon.* For, as Max Horkheimer and Theodor Adorno wrote in their essay, "The Culture Industry," "[a]ny need which might escape the central control is repressed by that of individual consciousness" (2002, 95). Yet, in imagining an interior, privatized place where dissenting views can only be expressed symbolically and ritually, "religion" also offers an opening—meager, though real nonetheless—to marginalized groups struggling to maintain some semblance of political autonomy in the face of an overwhelming *status quo.* As Adorno writes elsewhere, "activism is tolerated only because it is viewed as pseudo-activity [which is] the attempt to preserve enclaves of immediacy in the midst of a thoroughly mediated and obdurate society" (2002, 200–1). So long as oppositional acts can remain at the level of pseudo-activity— what the scholar of religion might classify as domestic rituals or symbolic behavior in contradistinction to public, political activity, or what the literary critic Stanley Fish names "surface pieties ... abstractions without substantive bite" (2002, 38)—it is greeted as, in Adorno's words, mere theater and thus tolerated.[8]

In offering this critique I hope it is clear that I am simply trying to chronicle what Clifford Geertz has already drawn to our attention:

> the conception of "Islam" being so desperately built up before our eyes by professors, politicians, journalists, polemicists, and others professionally concerned with making up our minds will be of great importance in determining what we do. (2003b, 39)

This is true across all the political divides: differing conceptions of "Islam"— as with the representations of any mass movement—play an explicit role in organizing all sorts of actions. For instance, it is not difficult to read the interviews that Osama bin Laden gave to US journalists in 1998 and 1999, let alone the writings of other far more conservative, so-called Islamic fundamentalists (for instance, take the writings of the Egyptian, Sayyid Qutb [1993], who was intent to rediscover the originary form of Islam but whose political program conflicted so drastically with the Egyptian state that he was executed by the Nasser government in 1966 [see Lincoln 2003, 3–5, 14–16, 60; McCutcheon 2003, 284–85; and Euben 1999, 53–55) and find the same rhetorical moves, used to authorize an obviously different sense of Islam from that of, say, such liberal commentators as Armstrong.[9] In fact, in his analysis of the speeches of George W. Bush and bin Laden, Bruce Lincoln has persuasively demonstrated that the same techniques are used by each rhetor to authorize their obviously different political positions (Lincoln 2003, 19–32).[10]

So, in agreeing with Geertz concerning the representation of Islam being built right before our eyes, I also join Fish in asking, "Who is it that is authorized to determine which version of Islam is the true one?" (2002, 35). For both my Chicago cab driver's and Geertz's portrait of Islam as a once peaceful and idle "faith" that has somehow been cruelly hijacked by a bunch of Islamist hooligans is not a value-free description. Instead, like all representations, it is a loaded prescription that functions behind the scenes, as with the work of Hollywood's production designers or an artist's authentication board. Such prescriptions are a potent rhetorical ploy that, in the case of writers such as Geertz, Rushdie, Esposito, and Armstrong, sanctions a very specific sort of politically liberal form of Americanized or, for want of a better term, compliant Islam open not only to the values of modern, free market investment, private ownership, and liberal democracy, but, more specifically, open to the US's unrivaled power to have its national interests direct the course of global events. It likely needs to be said that whether or not I happen to play by the particular socio-economic rules that characterize so-called modernity, whether or not I happen to agree with liberal democratic values or wish my retirement savings to continue to grow due to the miracle of compound interest, is not really relevant to studying the manner in which these contingent rules are being normalized, to quote Geertz, "by professors, politicians, journalists, and polemicists, and others professionally concerned with making up our minds."[11]

If we recognize that Geertz is indeed correct to identify how a representation of Islam is being concocted right before our eyes[12]—whether or not he also recognizes that he is a member of the Authentication Board working to concoct a very specific sort of provenanced Islam in what is actually an unregulated political and symbolic economy—then it should serve us well to examine more closely the sites where this activity is taking place (everywhere from newspaper editorial pages to world religions classrooms) and the tools by which we are doing our constructive activity. With the latter in mind, I would argue that it is none other than the taxon which draws so heavily on the presumed split between the tranquil inner life of the apolitical spirit and the hectic outer life of political conflict and contest. For, as already indicated, despite Geertz suggesting that, when trying to understand Islam, "we are left to find our way through vast collections of strange and inconsonant particulars without much in the way of assistance from finely drawn, culturally ratified natural kinds" (2003b, 36), the longstanding distinction between religion and politics—between faith and practice—that comes encoded in our modern category "religion" provides these pundits with considerable assistance in domesticating the "strange and inconsonant particulars" that confronted many people so startlingly on that morning of September 11.

As was so apparent on my own campus, when labeled as a "civilization," Islam is thought to be a rather homogenous thing that is in opposition to other so-called civilizations. For example, according to the often-cited Samuel P. Huntington, "Islamic 'fundamentalism,' commonly conceived as political Islam, is only one component in the much more extensive revival of Islamic ideas, practices, and rhetoric and the rededication to Islam by Muslim populations. The Resurgence is mainstream not extremist, pervasive not isolated" (1996, 110). Although Huntington does proceed to discuss "the political manifestation," he does not distinguish this from an apolitical inner spirituality, as do other more liberal commentators; instead, the so-called upper-case Resurgence that promises to brew clashes with other civilizations, is manifested at countless cultural sites where the monolithic civilization's "values" are taught and put into practice. In fact, Huntington likens this so-called Resurgence to the Protestant Reformation, but not insomuch as both movements distinguish public action from inner piety (as we saw, a distinction Rushdie apparently wishes political Muslims would make more often); he juxtaposes these movements because both events were driven by such things as a "vision of the perfect society" along with a "rejection of the powers that be and the nation state" (p. 111). Contrary to Huntington, pretty much all commentators who classify it as a "religion" are in agreement that the thing we have come to know as "Islam" is comprised of an ahistorical and essential core that is supremely authentic and spiritual, as opposed to its merely secondary and thus derivative outer forms of expression that are, alas, all too fallible. That this rhetorical distinction can serve many masters should be obvious by now; after all, as is apparent from even a casual listen to the rhetorics of actors on all sides of the political divide, this technique can be put to work authorizing virtually any position. The utility of this rhetoric of essences, then, lies not in its ability to single out what Armstrong confidently refers to as Islam's "hidden divine kernel" (2000, xii), but, in enabling a group—any group whatsoever—to portray its own ad hoc, and by definition contestable, interests *as* an unquestionable and thus divine kernel.

It is crucial to recognize that, insomuch as this artful technique is successfully employed in making a space for certain forms of marginal groups within alien and potentially hostile social environments—in a way that does not threaten but, instead, is seen to strengthen the dominant group by enabling its members to understand themselves as pluralistic and open— it should be more than obvious that such success is, ironically, evidence that the newly integrated minority groups have necessarily succumbed to a larger hegemony (in our case, free market liberal democracy) insomuch as they have had to rethink and retool their own group identity and sense of self, in the process privatizing and internalizing that which previously had been public and taken for granted. But, as already suggested, there are real (if tightly circumscribed) material benefits that come with such ghettoization. As the social theorist Immanuel Wallerstein has commented in the case of the historic beginnings of the political tradition we today know as liberalism, "[i]t came to be realized that *repression*, to be effective, had to be combined with *concessions*" (2000, 419; emphasis added)—what Said termed the process of simultaneously "enabling and disabling" (1997, 10). These concessions are specific, of course; much like Adorno's notion of pseudo-activity, they must not threaten the dominant group's practical interests yet must enable minority groups to put into practice their limited, self-perceived difference from their neighbors.

Regulating symbolic and political economies by means of repression/concession therefore cuts both ways. As this point is phrased by Fish, with regard to the artist's much-valued freedom of expression, "liberalism's disinclination either to authorize or condemn anyone's opinions" (as opposed to their organized action, of course),

> has provided the artist with his strongest bulwark against state regulation … but at the same time the argument deprives the artist of any rationale for intervening in precincts that have been assigned to other agents whose franchise is held no less exclusively than his. (1999, 36)

In making this point, Fish nicely draws upon the difference between how poetry—much like *pietas*—was once seen by earlier writers as a political force. For instance, take Philip Sydney (1554–86); in his *Defense of Poesy* (1595) he "authorizes poets … to intervene in public affairs" (Fish 1999: 35), whereas poetry today is understood as emotionally pleasing and thus politically irrelevant—succinctly summed up by Fish with the words, "who *cares* what poets do." This aestheticization, and this repression, of speech means that a contemporary reader is hard pressed to figure out why, for example, Plato was so concerned with the role of the poets in his ideal state's educational system. So, along with this repression—in our case, the domestication of potentially oppositional forms of political practice and social organization within the confines of supposedly private sentiment and pseudo-activity—comes a very real and, I would imagine, valuable concession, not to be minimized or dismissed: as phrased by Fish, when the revolution comes the heads of the poets will not necessarily roll along with that of the King, his ministers, and advisors. I think here of the widely reported phenomenon of cab drivers in such large cities as New York who, immediately after September 11, prominently displayed US flags and flag decals on their cars (whether done "sincerely" is *not* the issue, for such a debate is yet lodged in the interior, intentional discourse rather than shedding light on wider political processes).[13] This display was undoubtedly a concession to their customers, thought to purchase for the cabbies—many of whom are stereotyped as recent immigrants to the US—a patriotic space presumably safe from sporadic reprisals against some members of US minorities reported soon after September 11. There are, it would appear, practical advantages to tightly wrapping oneself in the flag.

Because there are indeed practical benefits to those members of minority groups who, for whatever reason, wish to move in from the margins (to earn material reward, to increase social rank, to effect incremental political change by working on the so-called inside, etc.), the Orientalism thesis argued by Said—despite parts of it being obviously influential of this essay—is not completely accurate since it paints with far too large a brush. For it is not the case that contemporary pundits work "[t]o demonize and dehumanize a *whole culture* on the grounds that it is 'enraged' at modernity" (1997, xxxvi; emphasis added). The unflattering, monolithic portrait of Islam that comes from the pen of such contemporary writers as Samuel Huntington notwithstanding, Said's 1978 thesis is not necessarily incorrect, just a little dated. For, as argued by Bourdieu,

> [t]he level of aggregation will be highest when the classification is applied to a region of social space that is distant, and therefore less well-known—in the same way that a city-dweller's perception of trees is less clearly differentiated than the perception of a country-dweller.... [S]ocial agents use as their reference points in establishing social positions the figures typical of a position in social space with which they are familiar. (1987, 10)

Social affinity, and the ability to employ greater specificity in acts of classification, is thus proportionally related to the degree to which material and political interests are shared. Of course, a greater distance and thus a higher level of aggregation does not necessarily mean that the so-called exotic will be feared as a threat; it could just as easily lead to paternally conceiving the Other as alluring, as in Michael Chibnik's anthropological study of the invention of "traditional" Oaxacan wood carvings, in which "sellers know that crafts sell well when they fit into a romantic narrative that places maximum cultural distance between artisans and customers" (2003, 243).

As an example of Bourdieu's point, consider a recent story on National Public Radio (NPR), on what is known as Quantrill's Raid.[14] On August 21, 1863, during the US Civil War, William Clark Quantrill (b. 1837) led a group of approximately three hundred rebel sympathizers fifty miles west from Lee's Summit, Missouri, to the city of Lawrence, Kansas, where they killed more than two hundred men and boys, in front of their wives and families, setting the town on fire in the process. The conflict, which pitted so-called Missouri Bushwhackers who were pro-slavery against the anti-slavery "free-staters" in Lawrence, involved Quantrill's men going door to door, over the course of several hours, killing, looting, and burning homes.

Although the US Civil War is yet a recent memory for some people, notably some of the descendants of those who were on the losing side—for whom it might be known as the War between the States or the War of Northern Aggression—it is probably fair to say that for many Americans it is now ancient history. The issues and grievances that prompted the conflict have little relevance today and the deep feelings of alienation and disenfranchisement that were likely shared by a number of people 140 years ago have by now dissolved into feelings of affinity and shared experience. Following Bourdieu, then, we could say that this is why, in its August 21, 2003, news story commemorating the 140th anniversary of the raid, NPR was able to produce what we could only call a balanced story on the raid that did not attribute culpability but, instead, emphasized moral ambiguity. After describing the event, the reporter, Greg Allen, interviewed residents on both sides of the Missouri/Kansas border, making clear to the listener that while it was indeed—in the words of a Kansas high school teacher and local historian whom he interviewed—"an atrocious event … that's hard for us to imagine today," for members of the Quantrill Society across the border in Missouri, the raid's leader

> was a hero here to the people here in Jackson County. If it wasn't for Quantrill, it might have been a lot worse. I mean people were treated bad enough, anyway, as it was. But they did have somebody to stand up for them and that was Quantrill.

By the end of the story, listeners understand that at this time Missourians were not only attacking Kansans across the border, but that Kansans were also attacking Missourians across the border, that parts of Missouri were occupied by Federal troops, and that Missourians felt like they had little choice but— using a phrase reminiscent of George W. Bush's "with us or against us" State of the Union address—to support Quantrill or, as one interviewee phrases it, "leave the state."

If by this point the ambiguity of the situation had not sunk in for NPR listeners, the fact that the story ends by making plain that Quantrill today possesses both celebrity and notoriety—that he is seen as a war hero who rightly deserved a full military burial when his bones were returned to Kansas in 1992 while yet being seen as a murderous criminal by others—ensures that listeners are prevented from reducing this historical episode to easy formulae and simplistic juxtapositions of good guys and "evil ones." Given the degree to which most of the radio listeners likely feel they share essential traits with members on both sides of this old and local political divide, they are capable of entertaining fine degrees of nuance in understanding the historical event. Not so when it comes to understanding those political actors with whom we have little or no affinity. That virtually no US mass media outlet has yet been able to seriously entertain that those people who participate in organized violence directed against US interests (both domestic and overseas) might have what at least they consider to be legitimate grievances—whether or not one legitimizes these grievances by agreeing with them—is evidence that for both ancient or current in-group conflict there is a luxury of empathy that group members clearly do not have when it comes to examining current conflict with non-group members. While NPR can paint Quantrill's raid with a fine brush—recovering historical details as they are seen from differing perspectives, details that prevent us from simply demonizing him a terrorist—it is utterly impossible for the same listeners to consider that, much like Missouri residents so long ago, today's suicide bombers (in such places as Israel, Sri Lanka, and now Iraq) may also feel between a rock and a hard place, left with little option but to make weapons of their own bodies in order to help achieve their group's material interests. Our lack of affinity with them allows us to overlook the details, so we simply understand them as demented, crazy, fanatical fundamentalists.

With Bourdieu's thoughts on affinity in mind, we return to Said's thesis in *Orientalism*, which was concerned with early-modern (eighteenth- and nineteenth-century) contact between Occident and Orient (in which the latter was homogeneously portrayed as the mysterious Other); perhaps it is the case that now, at the dawn of the twenty-first century, a far higher degree of social integration and incorporation—what sometimes goes by the name of globalization, Americanization, or, most critically, the now firmly established hegemony of late capitalism—has taken place such that sufficient affinities and shared material interests now exist across groups whose members, as with the US's north and south, once might have understood each other as mortal enemies. If this is the case, then it is no longer accurate to conclude, as Said once did, that "academic experts whose specialty is Islam have generally treated the religion and its various cultures within an invented or culturally determined ideological framework filled with passion, defensive prejudice, sometimes even revulsion" (1997, 6–7). That an ideological framework is still used is obvious; it is just that it is no longer sufficient to paint the entire culture with the same caricature. (As noted earlier, although no longer representative of a uniform portrait of Islam, we of course cannot overlook Huntington's influential generalizations, which carry such universal claims as "Muslims have problems living peacefully with their neighbors" [1996, 256]).

Instead, having a rhetorical toolbox that contains at least two caricatures (i.e., the contemplative, compliant mystic vs. the fanatical Islamist) is now far more useful for furthering a specific sort of integration in the interest of promoting one type of shared material interest. For "it is difficult to sustain the myth of Islam as an external Other ... [when] Muslim communities have spread throughout the western world, partly in response to economic demands for labour in the capitalist economies" (Turner 2002, 116). Contrary to an earlier stage in cultural contact (as noted by Richard Johnson, writing on Bush and Blair's anti-terrorist rhetorics), now there are "two kinds of Muslims in this discourse: there are good, loyal Muslims (loyal that is to their states) and bad Muslims who do not 'salute the flag'" (2002, 224).[15] As further evidence of this more recent development of shared material interests and social affinities, consider the words of Esposito, who begins his 2003 book, *Unholy War: Terror in the Name of Islam* by observing that "Muslims are our neighbors, colleagues, and fellow citizens." Now that this once alien "they" is recognized to be contained within the freshly expanded "our," there is an ongoing, collective project to "preserve our American values at home and abroad." To do this, "[w]e must be able to move beyond political rhetoric, beyond the world of black and white, or unadulterated good versus evil.… All of us are challenged to move beyond stereotypes, historic grievances, and religious differences, to recognize our shared values as well as interests, and to move collectively to build our common future" (2003, xi).

Because no coalition, no conception of "we," is static, lacking an authoritative, authentic, enduring core, pundits of differing political stripe have no choice but to continually work to normalize just those elements of diverse social movements that serve their own group's interests, picking and choosing along the way in their efforts to manage an ever-changing "our." As should be clear at this point, there are quite a few elements to the mass movement we know as Islam that are celebrated by those commentators who are, nonetheless, working to eliminate the problems posed by its so-called politicized aspects. As noted by Armstrong in her best-selling *A History of God*, commenting on early Muslim reform movements, "[t]he most popular solution was found by legists and traditionists who attempted to return to the ideals of Muhammad" (1993, 160). Sadly, she too fails to recognize that recovering some essential, originary ideal—in opposition to its ever-changing "external history"—is the tactic of choice for her as well! In this way, only specific portions of any particular marginal group need to be demonized since other portions—conveniently attributed to its timeless essence—inevitably fit rather nicely within the overall interests of dominant groups who control the means of representation. So, as argued by Turner, "[d]efining Islam as the foe [as well as the friend] has to deny or mask the wide range of distinctive cultural movements within Muslim societies.… The foe/friend distinction has to remain largely oblivious or indifferent to Said's modest observations about cultural hybridity and the futility of the Orient/Occident separation" (2002, 114, 116).

Whether willfully ignorant, oblivious, or merely indifferent, we now see a number of writers arguing that at its core Islam is a friend since there are liberal democratic values to be found in it. As Armstrong herself goes on to observe with regard to the nineteenth century, "Muslim reformers were not hostile to the West. Most found Western ideals of equality, freedom, and brotherhood congenial, since Islam shared the values of Judeo-Christianity which had been such an important influence in Europe and the United States" (1993, 362). Or, as recently argued in a far more ethnographically detailed study of the complexity of contemporary Turkish society, "Muslim societies in general, and Turkish society in particular, and their various sociopolitical movements have allowed a 'democratic space' to evince the same vital diversity and pluralism found in Western liberal democracies" (Yavuz 2003, ix). Even in a book such as Yavuz's, in which the author goes to great lengths to persuade the reader that the view of Islam as homogenous—whether across the globe or in one nation, such as Turkey—is theoretically unproductive (p. 34), we nonetheless see the same old assumptions regarding politics as being the expression of an interiorized faith that needs to be "flexible" in order to adapt to the demands of ever-changing external histories. Much as Wilfred Cantwell Smith once maintained, Yavuz argues that "one needs to focus on 'the individual Muslim actors, knowledgeable human agents who are possessors and strategic utilizers of local Islamic knowledge'" (p. 35; quoting Shahrani [1991, 182], whose essay is concerned with answering the question: "how have the basic principles and ethos of Islamic faith been socially produced, reproduced, and sustained?" [p. 162]). Despite the recommendation to think locally—something also recommended by Talal Asad in the opening chapter to his influential book, *Genealogies of Religion* (1993)—we are nonetheless left presuming that such a grand thing as "Islamic knowledge" or "Islamic faith" exists, only to be manifested in specific historic instances. Somewhat ironically, then, the politics of isolated, "local" actors apparently draws on a homogenous thing: "its repository of Islamic symbols for framing social and political issues" (Yavuz 2003, 35).

That even ethnographically precise studies nonetheless draw on the rhetoric of tradition suggests that the benefits of the repression/concession process are great indeed. For not only are they felt by marginal groups that are allowed to exist, in some form, within the so-called big tent; dissenters, when they dissent *properly*, help to ensure that members of the dominant group understand themselves as generous, well-intentioned, accepting, pluralistic, and thus tolerant. As most recently phrased by US Democratic Senator, Patrick Leahy, on a jacket blurb for Sunstein's book, "dissent is not merely an individual right, *reasoned dissent* and *balanced debate* are the very essence of a healthy, democratic society" (emphasis added) A passive-aggressive rhetoric betrays itself at this point, for in the apparent celebration of dissent it is controlled rather tightly. As Leahy's loaded comments concerning "reasoned dissent and balanced debate" make clear, much more than actual dissent, it is the *appearance* of a certain type of dissent that is the essence of a liberal democracy. Dissent works, is tolerated, is even celebrated, only if it is theatrical, pseudo-dissent, only insomuch as one disagrees or even opts out within very clear lines, continuing to play by a specific set of rules that inevitably reproduce divisions of power and ownership crucial to dominant socio-political arrangements.

For example, insomuch as he is sometimes said to be "beyond the gods," the Indian *sannyāsin* (renunciant) certainly dissents—no doubt dramatically—but it is the drama that is the key, here, for it is a dissent that is firmly privatized in the isolated biological individual, thereby not threatening the wider workings of an elaborate system of deference and privilege. Before proceeding we should note that it is no doubt significant that the image of a Hindu renunciant that dominates the popular imagination is that of a lone, individual ascetic deeply trained in meditation. Of interest, then, are the ascetics of the Mahanirvani Akharas, as observed by my former colleague, Jack Llewellyn, when he attended the 1998 Kumbh Mela pilgrimage in India. Though naked, these *sadhus* traditionally carry large weapons (such as axes and swords) and have a long-standing reputation as hired mercenaries. But of course this historical fact flies in the face of popular wisdom about the other-worldly piety of so-called religious people. They're just the wrong type of deeply faithful people.[16]

With the lone acetic in mind, when one considers the role food offerings play in the Hindu system of sharing merit, the renunciant's dissent is a crucial element in reproducing an elaborate system of social rank and exchange. "The master discourse," writes the theorist of visual arts, Victor Burgin, "organises the field of the generally permissible, in terms of what, in its terms, is *thinkable*.... [T]he master discourse is always already *in place* to receive its novices" (1990, 158). (Of note is that Burgin, whose work was brought to my attention by my colleague, Tim Murphy, distinguishes between debate and dissent, whereas Leahy's quotation makes clear that even the concept of dissent can be domesticated, such that its binary opposite is no longer "debate" but, perhaps, "criminality." Although, along with Burgin, one can attempt to recover the earlier, critical sense of dissent, simply saying "no" and thereby opting out, much as seen in the case of a 1960s hippie, reproduces the dominant discourse nonetheless.) Or, as made clear by the scholar of religion, Bruce Lawrence, in the opening to his book on fundamentalism, "the modernist paradigm ... envelops its dissidents as well as its advocates. Fundamentalists may protest, but their modernist adversaries, by domesticating their protests whether through media or the academy, try to reduce the autonomous power they project." As he goes on to conclude: "Domestication takes place at many levels" (1989, 7); although I agree, I would add one caveat: presuming that so-called fundamentalists have "autonomous power," and are doing something different from everyone else in society—i.e., working to actualize a picture of the world that entrenches each group's material interests—is but one more level of this combative process of domestication.

With the topic of domestication in mind, take a less controversial case that is a little closer to home: despite being demonized by elements of the corporate world, the much-celebrated consumer advocate turned 2000 Green Party Presidential candidate—and independent candidate in 2004— Ralph Nader, has long played a pivotal role in helping the free market system to work better (from the consumer's point of view), rather than attempting to overthrow it. Should dissent take the form of organized action outside of the so-called free market against, say, the commodity system that results from private ownership—instead of taking the form of Congressional hearings on the safety of the commodities—then this will no doubt be understood as an insurrection, possibly even a revolution, and the full might of the nation-state's system of coercive violence will be brought to bear on such fanatics and terrorists. For instance, think of the difference between, for example, the far left US contemporary film maker, author, and critic, Michael Moore, and the anti-Vietnam war activist, Jerry Rubin (1938–94), a member of the so-called Yippies. As phrased by MacFarquhar,

> [t]he Yippies were making fun of institutions so large that they were almost abstractions: they were mocking not Lyndon Johnson but the Presidency; not the head of the Stock Exchange but capitalism in toto.... For Moore, though, everything is personal. He's not angry with capitalism, or even with companies, he's angry with Roger Smith, the C.E.O. of General Motors, and Philip Knight, the C.E.O. of Nike. (2004, 140)

Although members of the nation-state are prevented from the unbridled pursuit of their own interests (hence experiencing a repression, though qualitatively different from that which is experienced by marginal group members), the concession purchased by means of tolerating, even encouraging, theatrical displays of toothless dissent is that people who are, by definition, placed all along a wide continuum of group membership can all be convinced that there *is* a truly free market and thus that they each have opportunities to hope for. They are persuaded that there exists a truly level playing field where all comers can freely mount the soap box in the town square and speak their piece (as pictured on Sunstein's book cover) and that their own group's practical dominance is the result of an unregulated free trade in ideas. Appealing once again to Burgin, we could say that "[t]he discourse allows the fiercest debates (as proof that it is open and spontaneous) but cannot recognise dissent" (1990, 158). That the deck is stacked in their favor, that their privilege is not the result of their individual merit, their disciplined work ethic, or the internal momentum of their superior ideas, and that only pseudo-opposition is allowed into the tightly regulated public sphere, goes utterly unnoticed by members of dominant groups. "Reasoned and balanced" dissent is thereby linked to self-satisfaction; contrary to Sunstein's conception of dissent pressing the free market of ideas in directions normally prevented by an unproductive, even lazy, consensus, *that's* precisely why societies need dissent.

Deeply held oppositional beliefs that are intimately related to practice and social interests are just the wrong type of dissent. As Fish ironically observes: "The only good belief is the belief you can wear lightly and shrug off when you leave home and stride into the public sphere" (2002, 37).

6 That Versatile Little Problem-Solver

Like it or not, techniques of repression of, and concession to, various forms of dissent operate most elegantly in liberal democracies; in return for gaining entry into the economic and political mainstream of liberal, free-market democracies (what many commentators simply refer to as "modernity"), peoples from all over the globe have had to ensure that their differences relative to the dominant group are largely internalized and practiced only within the confines of their hearts and minds—as the old saying goes— finding limited public expression in their so-called "ethnic" cuisines and their colorful "ethnic" costumes. For instance, whenever the topic of school prayer is raised in the US, as is often the case in the US south (where I happen to live and work), there is never any thought that promoting prayers once again in publicly funded schools might mean the appearance of a young student on his knees facing Mecca several times throughout the course of the school day, let alone the various other human behaviors quite reasonably classified as "prayer." (A point made also by Martin Marty [1995].) While most everyone in the US knows that it is a pluralistic state, this pluralism is somehow thought only to comprise the symbolic behaviors of minority group members (evidence of the useful split of theory from practice), who put it into practice only in a ritual fashion behind the closed doors of various sorts of domestic and voluntary associations. Difference thus resides in the private self and is manifested in such disembodied, symbolic behavior as cuisine or style of dress, while conformity of practice rules in all public affairs. For only dominant groups get to engage in praxis. In fact, when it comes to the members of dominant groups, "[w]hoever restricts himself to thinking but does not get involved is [seen by their peers as] weak, cowardly, and virtually a traitor" (Adorno 2002, 199); yet members of marginal groups who have little choice but to act differently than they profess to believe (e.g., Mormons professing to believe that multiple marriages for men are mandated by God yet recognizing that they are illegal under US law) are applauded by members of dominant classes for their integrity and principled behavior.

Elsewhere (2003, 241), I have discussed the case of John Ashcroft, President George W. Bush's Attorney General, and his Senate confirmation hearing in January 2001, at which he professed his religiously-based belief that abortion was a sin but, nonetheless, swore to uphold the "laws of the land" if appointed to office. Rather than seeing this as a mark of a hypocrite or someone whose beliefs are mere political conveniences, he was celebrated as a man of deep conviction and his nomination was confirmed.

But consider the more recent and, for me, at least, the more local case of the state of Alabama's Attorney General, Bill Pryor, who was recently appointed to a position as a US federal judge. While his nomination was making its way through the confirmation process (with federal Democrats dragging their feet in an attempt to prevent Pryor's appointment), the Chief Justice of Alabama's Supreme Court, Roy S. Moore, challenged the Constitutional separation of Church and State by having a large (two and a half tons!) monument to the Ten Commandments installed one night in the lobby of the state's Supreme Court office in Montgomery, a monument in the shape of an open book that also bears inscriptions around its base that make reference to other so-called historical documents and foundations of US law (e.g., the Magna Carta). After multiple court cases over the monument, in the summer of 2003 Moore was ordered by a US federal judge to have the monument removed but he did not comply. In early fall of 2003 the US Supreme Court declined to hear the case. In the meantime, after his own unsuccessful nomination hearing for a position on the 11th Circuit Federal Court of Appeals (at the July 31, 2003, vote he gained only fifty-three of the needed sixty votes for confirmation; another unsuccessful nomination was attempted later that fall[1]), Pryor seems to have had little choice but to make much of the fact that, although his personal beliefs agreed with Moore's actions (thereby sending an important signal to the like-minded), as the state's Attorney General he had no choice but to uphold the federal court order. For some in the state of Alabama, this is a distant cry from Pryor's widely quoted words at an April 12, 1997, rally in support of Roy Moore, then Circuit Court Judge of Alabama's Etowah County, when Pryor said that "God has chosen through his son Jesus Christ this time, this place for all Christians—Protestants, Catholics and Orthodox—to save our country and save our courts."[2]

Following the unanimous decision of Alabama's remaining eight Supreme Court Justices, ordering Moore to comply with the federal court order, Pryor released the following statement (August 21, 2003):

> Although I continue to believe that the Ten Commandments are the cornerstone of our legal heritage and can be displayed constitutionally as they are in the building of the Supreme Court of the United States, this controversy is no longer one involving a debate in the federal courts. The Supreme Court of Alabama has now spoken and ordered compliance with the federal injunction. Under our Constitution, federal and state courts must respect the orders of each other.[3]

So, after having once defended Judge Moore—back in the late-1990s when Moore posted the Ten Commandments in his own county courtroom, prior to his November 7, 2000, election to the position of Chief of the state's Supreme Court—Pryor now found himself with little choice but to prosecute Moore before the state's nine-member Court of the Judiciary. After a one-day hearing, this ethics board removed Moore from office on November 13,

2003, finding that, in his official capacity as Chief Justice, Moore "did willfully and publicly defy a federal court order directed to him." Moore's appeals to this decision continued throughout 2004.

This is a fascinating example of the problem of how the rhetoric of private sentiment is, or is not, related to public action. For in the case of Alabama's Moore and Pryor we have the two options that are open to those who consider themselves to be on the outside of the mainstream: (i) disengage one's belief from practice by internalizing and thus silencing the former, and thereby allowing one to integrate within a larger group (perhaps Pryor hoped for a position on the US Federal Court?); (ii) assert the strong linkage between belief and practice, and thereby suffer the consequences if the group of which you claim membership does not constitute the majority (Moore, removed from his position as Chief Supreme Court Justice, is nonetheless celebrated among the local conservative Christian population, some of whom have consistently turned out for sometimes dramatic rallies that coincide with his various court dates).

Without speculating on the sincerity of the actors involved, both options are understandable: in the case of the former option, Pryor's tactic is being used either to promote incremental change (i.e., change from the inside, such as slowly making the US a more godly country and thereby recovering, or so the argument goes, its Christian roots) or a tactic that will bring the social and material rewards of becoming a member of the dominant group heralded for one's high principles (the possible element of tokenism here is hard to ignore). In the case of the latter, seemingly strident option, incremental change is certainly not the goal and neither is the aim to win the favor of the dominant group. If anything, Moore's aim seems to have been the exact opposite: to inspire a dramatic change, in part accomplished by means of securing his status, authority, and thus influence within a group that sees itself to be marginal to "them," whether they be "liberals," "northerners," or "atheists." Of course, the extent to which Moore is actually a member of a marginal group remains to be seen, since he is now rumored to be considering running for public office (e.g., a federal Senate seat or, as some had recommended, to fill the position of Attorney General vacated when Bill Pryor was eventually promoted to the federal bench) in either 2004 or 2006. Since a position on the Alabama Supreme Court is gained through a public election, his 1997 trial for displaying the Ten Commandments in his circuit courtroom certainly did not harm him when, in 2000, he successfully ran as the "Ten Commandments Judge" for election as Chief of the state's Supreme Court. So marginality is itself a relative thing: being seen as marginal in the sphere of federal politics has no necessary relation to one's status at the local level. In fact, candidates for the Presidency of the US routinely emphasize that they are not "Washington insiders"—their marginality apparently winning them the favor of voters.

But this episode deserves a second look. For, as part of his defense for his actions, Moore—whose place on the Supreme Court required him to swear an oath to uphold the state's Constitution—said that since acknowledging God was his duty as Chief Justice he could not obey the Federal Court order to remove his monument for it would have required him to break his oath of office. Given that the preamble to the state's 1901 Constitution reads:

> We, the people of the State of Alabama, in order to establish justice, insure domestic tranquillity, and secure the blessings of liberty to ourselves and our posterity, invoking the favor and guidance of Almighty God, do ordain and establish the following Constitution and form of government for the State of Alabama.[4]

And, immediately following, in Section 1: Equality and Rights of Man, it reads:

> That all men are equally free and independent; that they are endowed by their Creator with certain inalienable rights; that among these are life, liberty and the pursuit of happiness.

It therefore seems that, from at least one reading of the Constitution, Moore was not really proposing such a radical position when, the day after taking his office, he was quoted in *The Tuscaloosa News* that "God's law will be acknowledged publicly as I've always said" (July 16, 2001); for, given the Constitution that he swore to uphold, "invoking the favor and guidance of Almighty God" in a public setting seems a pretty reasonable thing for the Chief Justice to do as part of his official duties. The artful separation of private sentiment from public action—so prominently used by Alabama's Attorney General Pryor—seems unnecessary.

Yet things are never quite as simple as this, of course. First off, there is the issue of the US Constitution's authority over any one state's Constitution. Given the way in which Moore and his supporters used the "states' rights" argument, it seemed as if they failed to take into account the 14th Amendment—ratified by the state of Alabama on July 13, 1868—which in part reads: "No state shall make or enforce any law which shall abridge the privileges or immunities of citizens of the United States."[5] Ratified by the Thirty-ninth US Congress on July 9, 1868, after twenty-eight of thirty-seven states had ratified it[6]—roughly two years after the end to hostilities in the US Civil War, depending on how one dates the end of the war, of course—the Amendment ensured that states could not bypass the 13th Amendment, passed on December 6, 1865, which stated: "Neither slavery nor involuntary servitude, except as a punishment for crime whereof the party shall have been duly convicted, shall exist within the United States, or any place subject to their jurisdiction." Taking into account how the rhetoric of "states' rights" was used forty years ago in Alabama—as part of an effort by then-Governor George C. Wallace (1919–98) to prevent the federally-mandated racial integration of the Alabama public school system, all of which culminated in his infamous "school house door stand" on June 11, 1963, which symbolically attempted to prevent the first African-American students from registering at the University of Alabama—Moore's use of this same argument conjures up an era in the state's history that many today would just as soon forget, while at the same time more than likely communicating significant meaning for those who, for whatever reason, possibly harbor a generally unspoken nostalgia for the state's pre-Civil Rights days. So, despite the states' rights argument carrying no legal weight whatsoever, ensuring that it is a losing argument from the outset, it might turn out to carry sufficient symbolic value to make it a winning strategy in the long run; for the rhetoric of "states' rights" may turn out to carry significant weight, for those whose democratic duties are performed not in law courts but in voting booths.

Another complexity arises when one realizes that the portion of Alabama's 1901 Constitution that Judge Moore's proclaims himself to be upholding is pretty clearly at odds with what follows in Section 3: Religious Freedom:

> That no religion shall be established by law; that no preference shall be given by law to any religious sect, society, denomination, or mode of worship; that no one shall be compelled by law to attend any place of worship; nor to pay any tithes, taxes, or other rate for building or repairing any place of worship, or for maintaining any minister or ministry; that no religious test shall be required as a qualification to any office or public trust under this state; and that the civil rights, privileges, and capacities of any citizen shall not be in any manner affected by his religious principles.

In the midst of an assertion of conformity we find the rhetoric of principles once again creating room for a manageable degree of difference; that a transcendent being is the ground of the state seems to go without saying (at least according to the authors of the Preamble), yet when it comes to asserting the specific characteristics of this being, the mode of worshiping it, the implications of believing in it, etc., things are not as self-evident as they once seemed.[7] As with the manner in which vague claims about terrorists in hiding, "sleeper cells," and an "axis of evil" nicely allow those who employ this rhetoric to adapt their interests to changing political circumstances, enabling differing things to be treated as threats when the need arises, so too the wiggle-room made possible by this obvious Constitutional ambivalence is likely to be crucial if the Constitution is to work; it is an ambiguity more than likely necessary given the way in which a Constitution *qua* static historical artifact must take on the appearance of being alive and thus relevant by means of it continually being re-read and re-reinterpreted in the light of new, unforeseen circumstances in which it must continually be understood anew and artfully applied. And it is precisely this gap between a Constitution's normative recipe for how things ought to be and the contingent world's refusal to neatly package itself—all of which means that Constitutions and the bodies charged with interpreting and applying them must be capable of dealing with ambiguity and ambivalence—that was the downfall of Moore's seemingly principled, consistent position.

Much like Tarantino's Mexican whorehouse, then, to some people Moore's position *was a little more authentic than was really necessary.*

Whether the disjoint between belief and compliance eventually turns out to be beneficial to Pryor's long-term career,[8] it is clearly a strategy that can be of tremendous use in many situations. But—now returning to the issue of representations of Islam—having identified the utility of this rhetorical move, my goal was not to diminish and thus argue away the sadly horrific nature of the recent military attacks *and* counter-attacks, nor was it to take sides regarding the grievances that motivated such actions and reactions. It was not to question the intentions of assorted scholars or to impugn the reputations of such people as Quentin Tarantino's production designers, Andy Warhol's Authentication Board, William Quantrill, Judge Moore, or Attorney General Pryor; neither was my aim to question the integrity of many present-day people who identify themselves as sincere, devout Muslims, living throughout the world, who were no doubt deeply and justifiably horrified by the September 11 attacks (and counter attacks). But neither was it to jump on the bandwagon of criticism for those who engage in overt acts of violence, for, after all, considerable portions of my own tax dollars help to finance the production and deployment of our own mass weapons of violence. Instead, the goal of the preceding was to identify, in a painfully recent and therefore fresh episode in the violent history of social formation, the intimate, intertwined, yet largely unrecognized relations between the discourses on religion, faith, freedom, belief, civility, economy, global interests, and the use of coercive violence (whether used along with a so-called first strike or as part of a retaliation[9]). For, as the scholar of religion, Bruce Lincoln, has commented in his own study of the post-September 11th rhetoric, "words are weapons in the present struggle" (2002, 9). So, just as the US historian, Howard Zinn, has persuasively identified the manner in which "the language of liberty and equality" was effectively used in the colonies throughout the mid to late eighteenth century to "unite just enough whites to fight a Revolution against England, without ending either slavery or inequality" (2003, 58), this essay has argued that the rhetorics of apolitical, personal faith used by self-appointed adjudicators of authenticity are handy devices that assist in coaxing into existence a specific type of social formation in what is obviously a competitive—and at times dangerous—political economy.

As Said once remarked: "Labels purporting to name very large and complex realities are notoriously vague and at the same time unavoidable" (1997, 9). It is therefore the case that, as one writer has phrased it, "[g]iven the vast range of human societies contained under the label 'Islamic', any process of selection or exclusion must also entail distortion" (Ruthven 1997, v). Or, as phrased by Beinin and Stork,

today's Islamist thinkers and activists are creatively deploying selected elements of the Islamic tradition, combined with ideas, techniques, institutions,
and commodities of the present and recent past, to cope with specifically
modern predicaments. (1997, 4)

However, this process of selection is neither, as Ruthven immediately goes
on to suggest, the result of an isolated, individual author following his or
her own "instincts and prejudices," nor is the deployment only of select
elements of a mass movement something that just the pious tradition's so-
called fanatical hijackers are doing, as Beinin and Stork suggest. Neither
are the criteria of inclusion and exclusion merely matters of private tastes
and sensibilities, nor evidence of nefarious forces bent on undermining
the peaceful world order; instead, this unavoidable process of selection
is, as Said goes on to discuss, a mode of interpretation, an inevitable
component of all acts of representation accomplished by members of
social formations busily competing for their share of the material turf.
Recalling Donald Lopez's earlier quoted words concerning representations
of Tibetan Buddhism, to ask which representation is right is to have entirely
missed the point—like the recent US Senate hearings on what ought to
count as a legitimate Muslim military chaplain.[10] Debates over issues of
authenticity thus do not correspond to some stable standard but, instead,
are part of a systematic discourse linked explicitly to practical, political
interests, regardless what those interests happen to be. They are fueled
by this process of selection, essentialization, and interiorization. "[W]e
must be prepared to accept," Said writes in the concluding chapter to his
1978 landmark book, *Orientalism*, "the fact that a representation is *eo ipso*
implicated, intertwined, embedded, interwoven with a great many other
things beside the 'truth,' which is itself a representation" (1979, 272).[11]

I therefore see no better way to summarize the position being argued
here with regard to that representation we call "faith" than to quote Karl
Marx, who, over 150 years ago, correctly understood the rhetorical and
political utility of this rhetoric. Appealing to the success of the socio-
political reorganization of Europe that we today depoliticize by calling it the
Protestant Reformation, he concluded that the great victory of Luther was
not that he brought about a theological revolution but, instead, that he

removed the servitude of devotion by replacing it by the servitude of
conviction. He destroyed faith in authority by restoring the authority of faith.
He turned priests into laymen by turning laymen into priests. He liberated
man from exterior religiosity by making man's inner conscience religious.
He emancipated the body from chains by enchaining the heart. (Marx
1977, 69)

It is therefore not so much that individual subjectivity has become a
refuge adopted by religion in the face of secular modernity's relentless
assault—as the once-popular secularization thesis was phrased early on by

Søren Kierkegaard (who, much like Rushdie, felt he had little choice but to write in seclusion and, in the early years at least, with the benefit of a pseudonym)—but that the very presumption of a private subjectivity—said to be the authentic place of a faith that is somehow removed from the political fray—is the site to which public dissent is banished and where it has little choice but to take refuge. In taking refuge in this space of no place and of no time, it is thereby curbed, modified, and tamed. With this in mind, it should be pointed out that "curbing and modifying" Communism, instead of seeking to destroy it, was the Cold War-era recommendation of the noted scholar of Islam and well-known religious pluralist, the late Wilfred Cantwell Smith, as contained in the closing pages of his once popular little book, *The Faith of Other Men* (1972). That these words were so easily seen not as a political program but as the hopeful musings of a liberal Protestant theologian is precisely the point that needs to be reconsidered.

Much, then, as the late E. P. Thompson, the noted British historian of Methodism's relations to the rise of the English working class, once observed the manner in which "[e]nergies and emotions which were dangerous to the social order, or which were merely unproductive ... were released in the harmless form of sporadic love-feasts, watch-nights, band-meetings, or revivalist campaigns" (1980, 405), so too energies that are deemed marginal to the interests of the *status quo* within modern, liberal democracies are channeled inward and released within the tightly controlled confines of the undoubtedly sincere yet politically ineffectual thing we call faith, religion, principle, and spirituality.

If this is the case, if the discourse on religion is one that effectively accomplishes real, political work, then we will have to rethink everything from the manner in which the Reformation is commonly understood as a religious event inspired by theological controversies to our tendency to see modern efforts to construct a theology of religious pluralism as being well-meaning, spiritual labors that pertain to disputes over great ideas. Instead, we will come to see those who participate in the discourse on religion, origins, spirit, tradition, principles, calling, and faith not as learned pundits necessarily operating in a realm unto themselves, far removed from the messy worlds of bodies and party politics, but, instead, as busy social engineers, as astute political operatives, and as artful production designers— all of whom are working in the trenches to deploy and massage systems of classification that are useful in constructing a very specific type of world. It is a world in which we can remain friends only if—as this book's epigraph from Nietzsche makes clear—certain things are never said.

I am therefore arguing that one of the means by which we purchase a particular sort of thing we call civility is that old Hegelian chestnut concerning the inner momentum of a uniform Spirit unfolding—sometimes slowly, sometimes only partially—throughout contingent History by means of a coherent tradition. But, as in the case of tranquillity achieved through vodka consumption, such civility is purchased at an exceedingly high, and necessarily undisclosed, social and intellectual price, especially when the exchange takes place in the context of a university classroom or over the public airwaves. For in such a case there is no analysis of the competing interests that comprise all less than perfect nations. There is no examination of how supposedly timeless canons and originary principles are in fact the inventions of subsequent traditions, doing their intellectual labors with the benefit of hindsight and within competitive social economies of their own. Choosing not to tackle the tough historical issues means that a disservice is being done to those who consume this information, since scholars are using the same rhetorical techniques that we see in use across the groups they study, from so-called "fundamentalists" of any stripe to political and legal pundits who presume that a "close" reading of historical documents will somehow allow us to conjure up the true intentions of, say, the "framers of the Constitution." As phrased by The Beatles, this is the old "get back to where you once belonged" technique or the political myth of the eternal return of the same, what we might also refer to as "desperately seeking certainty" (Farber and Sherry 2002); it is a profoundly anti-historical and thus powerfully conservative strategy insomuch as it legitimizes a specific distribution of power and privilege in the here and now by assuming that some eternal verity "struts and frets his hour upon the stage" of contingent history. Coming out of a scholar's mouth, just as when it comes out of the mouths of those who use this technique to achieve a host of different ends, this common rhetorical technique is not innocent, for it makes possible particular ways of organizing and ranking empirical forms of practice.

Instead of trying to recover the authentic experience that is supposedly manifested in symbol and behavior, and instead of arbitrarily selecting just this or that historical moment as the normative one, scholars—unlike the participants in the groups we study—could instead be concerned with examining this selection process itself, trying to determine the laws that govern this economy of signification, scrutinizing the relationship between various sorts of group identities and how they co-exist (or not) by means of such intertwined pairs of concepts as subject/object, private/public, emotion/rationality, belief/practice, sacred/secular, spirit/body, church/state, and, most generally and importantly, religion/politics. My thesis, then, is hardly original: in the discursive space created by means of these sets of abstract ideals, practical worlds of meaning, action, and organization are created, negotiated, and repressed. There is therefore something significant at stake in our use of classifications; as such, there is much to be learned from their study.

Therefore, despite what is written in the books of many scholars, the approach that I am advocating is neither about that thing some people call "the sacred" or "the holy," nor does it take a normative stance on such matters as how the so-called private zone of the Church ought to interact with the public zone of the State (a concern of great significance to many writers in the US who are intent on policing the limits of their social group). It is concerned not with a description or interpretation of any particular religious thing, and it is not an attempt at building an explanatory theory of religion. Instead, it examines how it is that we come to form ourselves into just these specific selves—and the aggregations of selves we call groups—by means of certain rhetorical styles and conventions, by means of classifying, and thus containing, parts of the observable world *as* religious in the first place. It argues that self-perception and self-understanding—the manner in which we are daily staked out as bounded entities—are the result of wider structural circumstances that, much like colorless vodka, a language's unspoken grammar, or the frame of a photograph, operate almost invisibly in the background, thus making very specific selves possible.

My interest thus is in a political theory of the category "religion." Presuming this thing we call reality to be what the essayist Joan Didion calls a phantasmagoria of disparate sensory stimuli, the scholar I have in mind studies the ordinary behavior, rhetoric, and narrative conventions that are routinely employed to tame this raucous collection of sensations, judgments, events, behaviors, coincidences, plans, accidents, values, and people, along with the ways in which knowledge, those who possess knowledge, and the things that are knowable by means of this knowledge, are organized, regularized, disciplined, and governed. We therefore study how people make do in their less than perfect groups. As Didion phrases it:

> We tell ourselves stories in order to live. We interpret what we see, select the most workable of multiple choices. We live entirely, especially if we are writers, by the imposition of a narrative line upon disparate images, by the "ideas" with which we have learned to freeze the shifting phantasmagoria which is our actual experience. (2001, 11)

This is none other than Musil's sense of a storyline amidst the contradictions. No wonder Popov concludes that vodka, and the illusion of freedom from the State that it produces, makes for better storytellers. He explains the long history of Russian writers who have had "a love affair with the bottle" by observing that "[v]odka makes it easier to think up literary plots" (Erofeyev 2002, 61). These are plots that concern the moment when subject and object, or private and public, become distinguishable, just as the messy phantasmagoria and the unruly past seem harnessed, if only for a moment, within discursive nets of our own making.

If you are with me so far then you might be able to entertain not only that the modern concept "religion" is but one means whereby we feel like we harness and steer the phantasmagoria in self-interested directions—thereby accomplishing just as much as we would had we taken just a few sips of vodka—but also that the uniform selves made possible by the presumption that such a thing as inner faith exists apart from its concrete historical setting are comparable to the meaning-making we accomplish only by ignoring a host of competing storylines.

Bringing to light some of the social and political utility that these specific sorts of selves hold for the modern democratic nation-state is therefore one possible goal for a fully retooled study of religion—or should I say "religion" in quotation marks? For this classification may be one of the best examples yet of what Sarah Vowell, that wonderfully ironic contributor to National Public Radio's "This American Life," likens to a soybean, "a versatile little problem-solver that can be processed into seemingly infinite, ingenious products" (2002, 5). Although she was speaking of the virtually limitless uses for the rhetoric of Abraham Lincoln's "Gettysburg Address," the modernist invention of the concept of religion, and the nation-state that comes with it, is just as good a candidate for the ironic title of "versatile little problem-solver." For the soybean that we call the category "religion" processes socio-politically enmeshed human beings into self-absorbed and seemingly disembodied believing minds, all the better for getting on with the business of living within those fractured worlds that comprise our day-to-day reality. For, according to Musil, we are all made up of ten characters: along with the first nine (comprised of everything from our professional self to our civic self and our sexual self) we also have "the passive fantasy of spaces yet unfilled," which is a tenth space that allows us not to take seriously what happens to our other nine characters (1996, 30). Much like Musil's sense of this "empty, invisible space" that allows us to be indifferent to history's unrelenting impact on us, like Nietzsche's silence that enables certain types of friendships, and just like tasteless vodka and the infinitely processable soybean, "religion" and "faith" are substantively empty, much like Marx's comment on Louis Napoleon's French election victory of 1848—"Just because he was nothing, he could signify everything" (Wheen 2001, 157). That is precisely what makes it so useful. Whereas Marx saw Napoleon as the man without qualities, for us "religion" is the category without qualities. Whether in academia, the courts, or on street corners, the discourse on faith, principles, authenticity, and belief act as but one cog in virtually any political wheel, making a particular world possible by allowing marginal groups to gain some sort of acceptance if only they idealize and privatize themselves, thereby simultaneously reproducing and putting up with the conditions of their own marginality.

I have tried to place before readers, for their inspection, our infatuation for understanding religion to be in opposition to politics, with the former being an item of inner sentiment, of private feeling, and of faith—a view aptly represented by US Supreme Court Justice Stewart who, writing the majority decision in the classic Abington v. Schempp school prayer case of 1963, stated that religion inhabits "the inviolable citadel of the individual heart and mind" (*Abington v. Schempp* [374 US 203 (1963)]). In asking readers to scrutinize this presumption, I hope to have shifted your attention from William James's well-known taxonomies of so-called religious experiences to studying the political utility of such taxonomies and the ways in which they are used by members of competing groups to portray their local, contingent interests as universal and necessary, thereby promoting one particular sense of the group while demoting all competitors.

In asking readers to consider making such a shift, I have requested that they entertain that the scholarly enterprise may play a key role in helping to reproduce the groups to which we belong, ranging from the academy to the nation-state. Simply put, can you call into question the presumption that the behaviors we as scholars study are somehow unique and set apart from the messy world of politics, making our object of study somehow distinct from the other mundane behaviors and memberships that occupy the daily lives of human beings. Because if you are able to historicize this pervasive assumption, then perhaps Willi Braun's recommendation will not sound as alien as it once might have. He writes:

> If "religion" is substantively empty—or infinitely fillable with aeolian qualities … [then] let us abandon the eschatological hope, so tenaciously persistent in our field, that by some brilliant hermeneutical can-do we will spook the true genie out of the bottle of "religion." If "religion" is substantively empty, then there is no genie in the bottle! (2000, 8)

If readers agree that there is no genie of presence in any conceptual bottle, then they might also be willing to entertain that those who continue to presume that religion refers to some real, internal, secret quality—whether they go by the name of historians, anthropologists, political scientists, sociologists, psychologists, etc.—may very well turn out to be some of the key players—those whom Chomsky names as ideological managers or Louis Althusser's professional ideologists, if you will—whose task is to reproduce the myth of privacy, the fable of the lone individual, and the illusion of free agency, all of which are necessary for the smooth workings of the modern liberal-democratic nation-state.

I have therefore asked whether readers can consider the very categories "religion" and "faith" defined in opposition to politics, defined as an item of inner feeling and private sentiment expressed and institutionalized in those semi-autonomous social sites we call mosques, temples, churches, or synagogues, to be a modern nationalist concoction, one that makes it possible to confect the specific sorts of selves we call citizens who, for the luxury of benefitting from their participation in *some* public spaces, internalize and repress their own dissenting voices. For, if we can entertain this, then we can understand how Žižek can move so easily from noting the post-September 11 appetite, among the reading public, to understand Islam "from the inside," to "redeem it" by seeing it to be "a great spiritual force," to the conclusion that, "[s]ympathetic as this attitude may be (and what is ethically more appealing than, in the midst of a violent confrontation, trying to put oneself inside the opponent's mind, and thus to relativize one's own standpoint?), it remains a gesture of ideological mystification *par excellence*" (2002, 34). Upon closer examination the appreciation of the depth of the Other's pure faith turns out to be, to borrow Žižek's wording once again, the "patronizing liberal respect for the Other's spiritual depth" (2002, 34). If this can be entertained, then our analysis of the workings of "religion" and the modern State will pick up where Althusser's work on ideology left off, for we will no longer see the institution of the Church to be among the Ideological State Apparatuses (1971, 152).

Building on his work, we will instead come to see that the very presumption that enables us to characterize the supposed semi-autonomy of an institution called the Church over against one called the State will itself be seen as the pre-eminent site where orderly (i.e., repressed and thus governed) people *qua* citizens are made; for it is just *this* presumption that is "the precondition for any distinction between public and private" (Althusser 1971, 144). For, as Žižek rightly understood, "[r]eligious belief … is not merely or even primarily an inner conviction, but the Church as an institution and its rituals (prayers, baptism, confirmation, confession …) which, far from being a mere secondary externalization of the inner belief, stand for *the very mechanisms that generate it*" (1997, 12). As Althusser's own example, adapted from Blaise Pascal's *Pensées*, fragment 250 (see Althusser 1971, 168; Althusser was using Léon Brunschvicg's numbering system),[12] is paraphrased by Žižek, "kneel down and *you shall believe that you knelt down because of your belief*—that is, your following the ritual is an expression/effect of your inner belief; in short, the 'external' ritual performatively generates its own ideological foundation" (1997, 12–13). This view does scandalously invert the dominant order of things, to borrow Althusser's own description of Pascal—a philosophically idealist order nicely represented in John Renard's *Seven Doors to Islam: Spirituality and the Religious Life of Muslims*, in which the religious life is understood as "the whole range of pious practices and creative endeavor *that is inspired by* and fosters spiritual growth (1996, xiv; emphasis added). Nevertheless, it applies Althusser's notion of interpellation to investigate the manner in which belief/behavior complexes allow biological individuals to be situated (to be recognized as, and to recognize themselves as) certain types of subjects (e.g., dissident, fanatical, freedom fighter, hero, soldier, innocent, guilty, etc.).[13] The Ideological State Apparatus most deserving of study is thus the very presumption—institutionalized at a variety of social sites—of an ironic split between belief and action, theory and practice, sacred and secular, with the former of each pair always presumed to be the inner, motive force, manifested in the latter term of each pair.

With all this in mind, then, we may offer an answer to the question posed in the subtitle of this book: "How to live in a less than perfect nation?"

Nurture the passive fantasy of an odorless, colorless, tasteless zone of apolitical contemplation that resides in people's hearts and minds and use it either as a site to safely act out toothless dissent while firmly ingratiating yourself to—so as to integrate yourself within—a larger hegemony, or as a place to safely contain what you see to be minor differences for the sake of forming a mass movement capable of replacing one set of imperfections with another that is more conducive to your own interests.

With this answer in mind, the reader is asked to look once again at the cover of this book, and consider the two mannequin-like figures, one seated and the other standing in the public town square. Perhaps they know what Nietzsche knew—that those intimate, local coalitions we call friendship are based on strategic silences. With no mouths, no ears, and no eyes they have little choice but to occupy their own silent and static interior world, making them ideal friends, orderly citizens, yet disquieted muses.

The fiction of faith thus makes selves more governable.[14]

Afterword

In the seventh season of "South Park" (episode #701)—the satirical cartoon series that is set in the fictionalized town of South Park, Colorado—the show's writers tackled the topic of the US's 2003 war with Iraq. With the town's adults evenly divided between vocal anti-war and pro-war protestors, Cartman—one of children known for his, shall we say, bad attitude and impolite behavior—was busy devising ingenious methods to avoid doing his homework on US history and, instead, was attempting to travel back to the time of the Founding Fathers. In a sequence meant to signify either a hallucination or his success at time travel, he arrived on the scene to witness the Continental Congress, embroiled in heated arguments of its own over whether to go to war.

In the midst of this debate, Benjamin Franklin speaks words of wisdom:

> Benjamin Franklin: "I believe that if we are to form a new country, we cannot be a country that appears war-hungry and violent to the rest of the world. However, we also cannot be a country that appears weak and unwilling to fight, to the rest of the world. So, what if we form a country that appears to want both."
>
> Thomas Jefferson: "Yes, yes of course, we go to war and protest going to war at the same time...."
>
> Benjamin Franklin: "And that means that, as a nation, we could go to war with whomever we wished, but at the same time act like we didn't want to. If we allow the people to protest what the government does, then the country will be forever blameless."
>
> John Adams: "It's like having your cake and eating it too."
>
> Anonymous Hick Redneck Founding Father: "Think of it: an entire nation founded on saying one thing and doing another."

There is no better way of summing up the preceding chapters, for this is precisely what the intertwined rhetorics of authenticity, spirit, principles, origins, and faith enable the members of groups—or better put, those large-scale groups we have come to know as nations—to do. They establish a social mechanism for uniform behavior to differ from competing and potentially contradictory intentions without ever attracting our curiosity, allowing us all to continue to believe in the existence of Meaning and Identity (the uppercase is purposefully used), despite the fact that everyone seems to think that everyone else has missed the point and is beyond the camp fire's warm glow. Being a citizen who is both an individual self and a node of the nation-state means that we need such devices to allow us—as opposed to them, of course—to have our cake and eat it too.

This is how we live in a less than perfect nation.

Endnotes

Chapter 1

1. For example, see the story broadcast in the US on February 18, 2004, on National Public Radio (NPR), "Iraq: A Case Study in the Roots of Genocide." An audio file is posted at http://www.npr.org/rundowns/rundown.php?prgId=3&prgDate=18-Feb-2004.

2. According to Canada's International Development Research Center, in Sri Lanka alone it is estimated that 48.5% of the deaths of all children under five are due to childhood diarrhea-related illnesses. See http://web.idrc.ca/en/ev-37946-201-1-DO_TOPIC.html.

3. Posted at http://www.christianchildrensfund.org/working_for_children/health/water/safewater.cfm and available in March 2004.

4. As phrased by Susan Sontag, in her recent short book, *Regarding the Pain of Others*, establishing such a thing as a Museum of the History of Slavery in the US (where there is currently no such institution), is likely not possible for it

> is a memory judged too dangerous to social stability to activate and to create. The Holocaust Memorial Museum and the future Armenian Genocide Museum and memorial are about what didn't happen in America, so the memory work doesn't risk arousing an embittered domestic population against authority. To have a museum chronicling the great crime that was African slavery in the United States of America would be to acknowledge that the evil was *here*. Americans prefer to picture the evil that was *there*, and from which the United States—a unique nation, one without any certifiably wicked leaders throughout its entire history—is exempt (2004, 88).

5. I have in mind the 1988 deaths of an estimated (according to Amnesty International) 5,000 Kurds in Halabja, in northern Iraq, by means of mustard and nerve gas as well as the Iraqi use of chemical weapons against Iranian troops (beginning in 1982) during the Iran-Iraq war (1980–88). Moreover, as was reported in the May 25, 1994, hearing of the US Senate Committee on Banking, Housing, and Urban Affairs 103-900 (concerning US Gulf War veterans' post-war illnesses, known as Gulf War Syndrome), Iraq obtained such agents as anthrax, VX nerve gas, West Nile fever, and botulism from the US throughout the 1980s. As cited in the Introduction to the report, the Senate hearing was prompted by post-Gulf War I "UN inspectors [who] identified many US-manufactured items exported pursuant to licenses issued by the US Department of Commerce that were used to further Iraq's chemical and nuclear weapons development and missile delivery system development programs." See the full hearing report posted at the site established by James J. Tuite, former assistant to the Committee Chair, Senator Donald W. Riegle Jr (the credibility of his site, and the legitimacy of the document posted there, can be confirmed by contacting the office of

the US Senate Committee on Banking, Housing, and Urban Affairs), at: http://www.chronicillnet.org/PGWS/tuite/2NDINDEX.HTM.

6. For example, the most scholarly of the three above-mentioned books on religious violence is Jurgensmeyer's; nonetheless, he understands such actions by distinguishing between practical or strategic violence (which is rightfully understood as political) and performative or exaggerated violence (which is symbolic and thus the choice of religious actors). On the difficulties with his typology, see McCutcheon 2003, 269–72.

7. See James 2002 for the "centenary edition" of the book, complete with sixty-three pages of new introductory material.

8. This opens what is known as Wittgenstein's "private language argument":

> What reason have we for calling "S" the sign for a *sensation*? For "sensation" is a word of our common language, not of one intelligible to me alone. So the use of this word stands in need of a justification which everybody understands.—And it would not help either to say that it need not be a *sensation*; that when he writes "S," he has *something*—and that is all that can be said. "Has" and "something" also belong to our common language.— So in the end when one is doing philosophy one gets to the point where one would like just to emit an inarticulate sound.—But such a sound is an expression only as it occurs in a particular language-game, which should now be described. (1968: 93e)

9. I take this to be an instance of cultural infantalization, which is widely present in US culture today. For instance, consider the fact that US news broadcasters now routinely employ English subtitles whenever an English speaker from elsewhere in the world is being interviewed, as if their US viewers are incapable of making sense of an English speaker from India or even Britain.

10. Unless otherwise noted, all of the following quotations are taken from the official transcript of the March 7, 2003, broadcast of the "Morning Edition" story entitled, "Church Resisting the Release of Documents that Detail Communication with Priests." For an archived audio version of the story, "L.A. Archdiocese Resists Releasing Documents," see http://discover.npr.org/features/feature.jhtml?wfld=1185490.

11. Of interest is that the privacy, and thus privileged autonomy, of this sacred relationship was not the only argument used by the archdiocese's lawyers. "In criminal and civil cases, lawyers for the archdiocese cited other privileges that would keep the documents confidential, including those involving attorney-client, doctor-patient, and penitential relationships" (Lobdell and Winton 2003, B6).

12. Regarding the role played by the IRS in determining the tax status of religious organizations, see the 2002 Ninian Smart Lecture, delivered by Jonathan Z. Smith, and posted at http://webcast.ucsd.edu:8080/ramgen/UCSD_TV/7910.rm.

Chapter 2

1. See McCutcheon 1999 for an introduction to how this methodological problem has been addressed by linguists, anthropologists, philosophers, and scholars of religion.

2. Segal's comment was made as part of a presentation he gave at the 1995 Congress of the International Association for the History of Religions, held in Mexico City, Mexico.

3. If the latter hypothetical title strikes the reader as being in particularly bad taste, then it is precisely this judgement that I wish such readers to scrutinize more closely, for the authority given to the participant self-report may very well have more to do with our political, aesthetic, or moral agreement or disagreement with the thing under study than it does with some self-evidently obvious nature of the thing itself.

4. Darnton's review essay focuses on the work of the late Donald F. McKenzie (d. 1999), well-known for his influential book, *Bibliography and the Sociology of Texts* (Cambridge University Press, 1999). One of McKenzie's contributions was made in his 1966 book (and former Cambridge University dissertation) entitled, *The Cambridge University Press, 1696-1712*, in which he did a detailed bibliographical study, relying on the press's own archives, of all books produced by the press during this period. Prior to him, the assumption that drove bibliographic quests was that "each book would move through the chain of production according to a consistent, linear pattern," therefore making it possible for contemporary scholars "to construct a series of inferences, moving backward through the production process from the physical copy, to a press, a compositor, and at least to some extent, the original manuscript, even if it were missing, as in the case of Shakespeare" (Darnton 2003b, 44). In light of McKenzie's detailed work, it was learned that the production process (and thus the basis for latter-day reconstructions or an *Ur*-text) was anything but coherent and linear—a finding that, in Darnton's estimate, "sounded innocent enough as an idea; but when he developed all its implications, he seemed to sap the foundations of orthodox bibliography."

5. While I realize that my position presumes that everything is an item of discourse—making "clay" and "shard" no more real, present, or empirical than "ancient pot"—I make the point in this manner to illustrate the historical problem entailed in presuming that the past is present. That even the present is not itself present—at least in the manner in which our folk ontologies routinely believe it to be, since the present can only be experienced through a complex series of cognitive and biological processes—must not go unnoticed, of course.

6. One of these canvases, dated "1918," is part of a private collection on display in 2003–2004 at the University of Iowa Museum, Iowa City, Iowa.

7. It should be said that this problematic makes apparent the presumption that being "educated" and "cultured" means one necessarily agrees with the observer's way of understanding the world.

8. See Dunn 1990 for an example of how this rhetoric is used to tame competing senses of early Christianity.

9. Recognizing the problems of how it is that we address the affective dimension, Lincoln coins the term "sociogravitational forces of attraction and repulsion that can be stimulated by discourse" (1989, 176 n. 9). What I particularly like about his neologism is that it helps us to avoid sentimentalizing sentiment and, instead, prompts us to see sentiment as a social, discursive artifact. I have in mind, here, the need for those interested in political analysis to avoid such things as Taylor's sentimentalizing of emotion, as outlined earlier in Chapter 1.

10. Thinking back to the opening anecdote, I should point out that the dramatic

difference in age between the student and Carl suggests a degree of condescension—
or what an ancient Greek might have termed impiety—on the part of the student.

11. As of 2001, this film series from 1977 is distributed in DVD format by
Ambrose Video Publishing, Inc., of New York.

12. But just where is the line? That explicit sexuality is far more prevalent in
popular culture than it once was (prime-time network sitcoms in the US routinely
premise their plots on such topics as strippers, homosexuality, masturbation, one-
night stands, extra-marital affairs, etc.), makes Janet Jackson's breast-baring incident
(with her nipple artfully covered, mind you) seem rather mundane.

13. See Goldschmidt's introduction to the co-edited *Race, Nation, and Religion
in the Americas* (Goldschmidt and McAlister 2004) for an example of a scholar
attempting to overcome the apparent imperialism of objective studies by trying
to dialogue with, as opposed to invalidate, participant disclosures. He seems to
overlook the fact that the human sciences have nothing to do with validation or
invalidation, let alone objectivity, but are instead comprised of a series of controlled
heuristics scholars use to study human behaviors.

Chapter 3

1. According to Nemtsov (2002), the mid to late 1980s anti-alcohol campaign
of Gorbachev's Soviet government reduced annual per capita alcohol consumption
and decreased all mortalities due to alcohol (e.g., not just poisoning but also
accidents caused by impairment, etc.) from 1161.6 per 100,000 people to 1054.
Despite estimating that, between 1986 and 1991, 1.22 million lives were therefore
saved, in 1994 alone there was a total of 751,000 alcohol-related deaths.

2. As reported by Erofeyev; to determine the contemporary value in dollars I have
used *Comecon Data*, produced by the Vienna Institute for Comparative Economic
Studies (London: Macmillan, 1989), 383; according to this resource, the conversion
factor for imports/exports lists one Ruble in 1975 as being equivalent to US $1.3862. I
also used the *Consumer Price Index* for 1975 (http://oregonstate.edu/Dept/pol_sci/fac/
sahr/cv2003.pdf), which uses a factor of 0.293 to convert US $1 in 1975 to $3.413 in
2003.

3. Just what gets to constitute normative Islam (let alone the normative form of any
mass movement), and hence the standard against which any particular understanding
can be judged a *mis*-understanding, is the question to be posed throughout the following chapters.

4. Lewis certainly follows Huntington in this regard. For instance, in Lewis's
What Went Wrong: The Clash Between Islam and Modernity in the Middle East (2003)
there are only three page references under "religion" in the index (though four
appear under "persecution, religious"). In fact, the trouble with this civilization, at
least according to such overly ambitious writers as Lewis, is that the religion/politics
distinction that apparently lies at the heart of Christianity—"render unto Caesar
the things which are Caesar's; and unto God the things which are God's" (Matt
22:21)—is absent in Islam (see Lewis 2004, 5–7; see also 2004, 97). Although this
characterization of Islam will be addressed below in greater detail, suffice it to say
for the time being that, in assuming that the spheres named as religion and politics

are ontologically distinct realms, writers such as Lewis fail to entertain that such Bible passages provide the social theorist with artifacts that constitute what I have elsewhere described as "a fascinating study in tactical, emergent social engineering" whereby "marginal or emergent social formations ... carve out a zone in which to exist" (2003, 272).

5. Although he argues that *dīn* refers to "the external forms this religion [i.e., Islam] took in combining worldly action with religious inspiration and thought" (2003, 106), Waardenburg's survey of the historical uses of the term is worth considering (pp. 101–7).

6. In fact, this is the manner in which *dīn* is translated most always—in older as well as modern editions. See, for example, the English translation by Fakhry (2002) and the French translation by Blanchère (1966).

7. Despite its mission to spread the word of the Christian God to the nations, I assume that the American Bible Society (ABS) seeks merely to translate the Bible into foreign languages and not to reorganize the text in a fashion more appealing to novice readers.

8. Although his work is but another example of the troublesome metaphysics of presence we find in this field, those interested in the etymology of religion would do well to consult chapter 2 of Wilfred Cantwell Smith's 1962 classic, *The Meaning and End of Religion* (1991; notably, chapter 2, "'Religion' in the West"). Other relevant English language resources on the history of "religion" range from W. Warde Fowler's early work (e.g., 1908, 169–75 and 1933, 319–52) to Toomey (1954), J. Z. Smith (1998), and Griffiths (2000).

9. The existence of the ossuary was first made public in the US at an October 21, 2002, news conference in Washington, DC, sponsored by *BAR*. For those not up on their recent biblical archeology discoveries, the ossuary of James is a limestone box about fifty centimeters long, twenty-five centimetres wide, and thirty centimetres high that would have contained a deceased person's bones (this form of Jewish re-burial was practiced from around the first century BCE to the destruction of the second temple by the Romans in 70 CE); the box bears an Aramaic inscription, about eighteen centimetres long, which, in transliteration, reads *Ya'akov bar Yosef akhui di Yeshua* ("James, son of Joseph, brother of Jesus").

10. This wonderful pun was devised by a student at the University of Alabama, John Parrish, who coined it upon hearing of Hershel Shanks's statement. I thank John for allowing me to use it.

11. A so-called authenticated artifact, of course, is one that has a certificate that documents where it was found, by whom, when, etc. What this has to do with reading the artifact back into some ancient history is, of course, rather more troublesome than the notions of a provenanced versus an unprovenanced artifact at first suggests. Also of interest is that the owner, Oded Golan, a fifty-one-year-old engineer and private collector who lives in Tel Aviv, at first was reported to have said he obtained the box fifteen years ago. He later corrected this, saying that although he had it in its current place for about the last fifteen years, he has owned it since the early to mid 1970s (in one report, he is even said to have purchased it in 1967 when he was sixteen). If the first version is correct—and Israeli Antiquities Authorities investigated this and determined that the artifact was not authentic—this would put his acquisition of the box well after 1978, the Israeli government's cut-off date for those who purchase or discover artifacts. According to the Antiquities Law of the

State of Israel of 1978 (5738-1978 [1]), if the purchase or discovery of an antiquity (defined in the Law as anything made by human beings before 1700) was made *prior* to 1978 then owners who have no receipt documenting that their purchase was made from a licenced antiquities dealer are allowed to keep their artifacts, no matter how they obtained them. However, post-1978 purchases and discoveries that cannot be documented become the property of the state of Israel (see Shanks 2003a, 22). On June 18, 2003, the Israeli Antiquities Authority pronounced the inscription a forgery. See http://www.cnn.com/2003/TECH/science/06/18/jesus.box/.

12. This is quoted from an brief article entitled "Conservation," which is itself part of the Royal Ontario Museum's web article, "The James Ossuary" (www.rom.on.ca).

13. Of course the historicity of the inscription was hotly debated. For example, as melodramatically reported by Shanks, at the 2002 meeting of the Society of Biblical Literature, Eric Meyers, of Duke University, "suggested that the ossuary's current owner … might have purchased it only recently and added the last two words ('brother of Jesus') to the inscription. Golan was sitting in the audience and Meyers looked straight at him" (2003b, 55–56).

14. As phrased in a web article by Stephen H. Sanchez, then a doctoral candidate at Dallas Theological Seminary: "The box is an archaeological find that is interesting because it may confirm some of the historical realities Christians already believe" (2002).

Chapter 4

1. Although the two previously cited books in part address scholarly and popular representations of Islam, it should not be forgotten that this is how all of those mass movements we classify as world religions are routinely treated. As my preferred term, "mass movement" should suggest, even labeling them as "world religions," and seeing such things as "Hinduism" and "Christianity" as obviously bounded, distinct social realities that cohere over time and place, may be part of the problem. On the history of the "world religions" concept, see Masuzawa forthcoming a and forthcoming b.

2. For the polling results, see http://www.washingtonpost.com/wp-srv/politics/polls/vault/stories/data082303.htm.

3. See the White House's site for a transcript of the brief question/answer period that followed Bush's September 17, 2003, meeting with the Congressional Conference Committee on Energy Legislation. A reporter asked:

> Q: Mr. President, Dr. Rice and Secretary Rumsfeld both said yesterday that they have seen no evidence that Iraq had anything to do with September 11th. Yet, on "Meet the Press," Sunday, the Vice President said Iraq was a geographic base for the terrorists and he also said, I don't know, or we don't know, when asked if there was any involvement. Your critics say that this is some effort—deliberate effort to blur the line and confuse people. How would you answer that?

> The President: We've had no evidence that Saddam Hussein was involved with the September 11th. What the Vice President said was, is that he has been involved with al Qaeda. And al Zarqawi, al Qaeda operative, was in

Baghdad. He's the guy that ordered the killing of a US diplomat. He's a man who is still running loose, involved with the poisons network, involved with Ansar al-Islam. There's no question that Saddam Hussein had al Qaeda ties. Posted at http://www.whitehouse.gov/news/releases/2003/09/20030917-7.html.

4.   In his response to a January 8, 2004, Carnegie Endowment for International Peace report that states that "there was and is no solid evidence of a cooperative relationship between Saddam's government and Al Qaeda" (see pages 7 and 48 of the report) and that criticized the administration's influence over, and, as phrased by the report, its systematic misrepresentation of, US intelligence reports (see pages 7, 50–53 of the report), it was reported that Powell said that although "he had seen no 'smoking gun, concrete evidence' of ties between Saddam Hussein and the al Qaeda terror network," he nonetheless "insisted that Iraq had had dangerous weapons and needed to be disarmed by force." The full CBS news story is posted at http://www. cbsnews.com/stories/2003/06/25/iraq/main560449.shtml?cmp=EM8707. The full Carnegie report, which was written between September and December of 2003 and entitled "WMD in Iraq: Evidence and Implications," is posted at http://wmd.ceip. matrixgroup.net/iraq3fulltext.pdf.

5.   Results and analysis of this December 15–16, 2003, joint poll was posted at http://www.gallup.com/poll/releases/pr031219.asp (in February 2004). Subscribers of their service can now access the poll results at: http://www.gallup.com/content/ login.aspx?ci=10054.

6.   The forty-seven minute audio file (along with a video file) from this press conference, "President Bush Holds Press Conferences," is posted at http://www. whitehouse.gov/news/releases/2003/12/.

7.   Posted at http://www.msnbc.com/news/966470.asp?cp1=1.

8.   Posted as an audio file at http://www.npr.org/display_pages/features/feature_ 1610113.html; a longer version of the interview, not played in its entirety on the radio, is also posted.

9.   Posted in March 2004 at http://stacks.msnbc.com/news/962627.asp.

10.   The full text of these remarks, along with questions from reporters, is posted at the US Department of Defense's site, http://www.defenselink.mil/speeches/2002/ s20021018-depsecdef.html. I am indebted to Powers' hard-hitting critique of what is now clearly the Bush administration's highly questionable case for war (2003) for bringing this speech to my attention.

11.   Posted at http://www.whitehouse.gov/news/releases/2004/01/20040120-7.html.

12.   Posted at http://www.pipa.org/OnlineReports/Iraq/Media_10_02_03_Press. pdf; see the questionnaire, bearing the URL suffix 10_02_03_Questionnaire.pdf, as well as their report, bearing the URL suffix 10_02_03_Report.pdf.

13.   In saying this I wish not to ignore the pain that resulted from the September 11 attacks; I do, however, wish to draw attention to the ease with which our own social group engages in mass-scale violence in other nations.

14.   According to DeMott, his proposal for a "twenty-first-century political shit detector" can help to identify five characteristics of junk politics, the first two of which are that it "personalizes and moralizes issues and interests rather than clarifying them" and that it "takes changelessness as a major cause—changelessness meaning zero interruption in the processes and practices that strengthen existing, interlocking systems of socioeconomic advantage" (2003, 36).

15. With the US's eighteenth century in mind, consider the juxtaposition between Darnton's recent book, *George Washington's False Teeth: An Unconventional Guide to the Eighteenth Century* (2003a)—which emphasizes the chronological distance and cultural strangeness of this period when compared to contemporary life in the US— and a recent magazine ad for the tourist site, Colonial Williamsburg, in the state of Virginia, where "time stands still." The ad goes on: "Here, you're an active participant in a vibrant 18th-century society, full of impassioned citizens, talented performers, and limitless possibilities. Come prepared for the time of your life." Having read "thousands of letters from people in all walks of eighteenth-century life" (p. 23), Darnton argues that, contrary to the rosy picture used to sell this tourist destination, a good portion of your life's time in Colonial Williamsburg would have been spent, and your passions focused on, either having or worrying about having toothaches.

16. Sontag explains that there exist two exposures of the valley through which Fenton, assigned in 1855 by the British government to photograph the war, thought the ill-conceived charge of the light calvary brigade had taken place. Although both were taken by him from the same position, in the first "the cannon balls are thick on the ground to the left of the road" whereas prior to taking the second, which ended up being the well-known image, Fenton "oversaw the scattering of the cannonballs on the road itself" (2004, 54).

17. For a recent discussion of the uncanny valley, see Dave Bryant's "The Uncanny Valley," posted at http://www.arclight.net/~pdb/glimpses/valley.html. The most cited discussion continues to be Reichardt (1978, 26–27). See also Mori's own thoughts on the relations between science and "the ultimate truth of the Buddha" (1999, 129).

18. See Catherine Milner's article "Collectors Insist 'Our Warhols are Genuine'" in *The Sunday Telegraph* (October 26, 2003). Those owners of one-time original Warhols who are contesting the Board's decision are currently preparing a lawsuit.

19. A fascinating study awaits the ambitious person interested in analyzing the marketing and publishing of books on Islam in the post-September 11 world. Such a study would examine everything from the hurried appearance of reprints, new cover art, and lightly revised second editions, to a newly acquired prominence of such books in ads and catalogues, as well as the rate of newly commissioned books, all of which needs to be linked to financial investment and profits and compared to the rate at which such information was produced in the US on the heels of the so-called Iranian hostage crisis (which lasted from 1979–81).

20. One must not forget that, in a variety of speeches in the mid-1980s, then-President Ronald Reagan routinely termed the Nicaraguan Contras "freedom fighters."

21. I am indebted to Paul Johnson (2002) for bringing Rushdie's article to my attention, which was also quoted in McCutcheon 2003, 242.

22. Posted at the British government's official site: http://www.number-10.gov.uk/output/Page1606.asp.

23. Posted at http://www.number-10.gov.uk/output/Page1615.asp.

24. Posted at http://www.number-10.gov.uk/output/Page1634.asp.

25. Posted at http://www.whitehouse.gov/news/releases/2001/09/20010917-11.html.

26. Posted at http://www.whitehouse.gov/news/releases/2001/09/20010920-8.html.

27. As phrased by Bryan S. Turner: "Protestantism had weakened the importance of the public domain through its emphasis on individualism and privacy. The Protestant ethic was manifest in modern liberalism that had promoted a retreat from the social world" (2002, 107). This having been said, it must be noted that classifying this as a specifically religious development—insomuch as Protestantism is widely understood as a religion rather than as a mass political movement—is part of the problem this essay seeks to address.

28. As background: Barnett Slepian, an obstetrician/gynecologist, was fatally shot by what police described as a sniper in his home in Amherst, NY, late on the evening of October 23, 1998. James Charles Kopp, with a long history of anti-abortion activities, soon became the subject of an FBI manhunt in the US and was also charged by Canadian authorities with the shooting (not fatal) in 1995 of Dr Hugh Short, a gynecologist, in his home in Ancaster, near Toronto. In March 2001, Kopp was arrested in France, eventually returned to the US, tried, and on March 18, 2003, he was convicted of murder. And, on February 25, 1994, Baruch Goldstein—a thirty-eight-year-old Brooklyn, NY, physician, immigrant to Israel, and so-called Jewish settler—used an automatic rifle to kill Muslim worshipers during Friday prayers, and then kill himself. Hebron, a West Bank city largely populated by Palestinians, has long been a disputed city since, in both Jewish and Muslim mythologies, it plays a significant role, being the site where it is believed that Abraham and Sara, among others of the so-called Patriarchs, were buried. A Jewish shrine and a Muslim mosque can be found at this site today.

Chapter 5

1. This has significant similarity to the argument of Tomoko Masuzawa concerning the study of religion's ambivalence toward its own speculative quest to determine the origins of religion (a quest that was characteristic of the nineteenth-century scholarship of such writers as E. B. Tylor and James G. Frazer), on the one hand, and, on the other, subsequent scholarly interest in exclusively studying groups who devote their social energy to a discourse on origins. She concluded that the early-twentieth-century's turn away from a speculative quest for origins has nonetheless been vicariously accomplished through the preoccupation with studying groups who themselves claimed to have access to the time of the ancestors (Masuzawa 1993; see also Masuzawa 2000b).

2. For readers not familiar with this episode, in early March 2001 it was widely reported throughout the European and North American media that large (approximately 35 to 50 meters tall), pre-Islamic Buddhist statues carved out of the sandstone mountains in Bamiyan province of north-central Afghanistan were destroyed by Taliban rockets and explosives. For one report see Radio Netherlands's site: http://www.rnw.nl/hotspots/html/afghanistan010302.html.

3. On the complex history of the term *jihād*, including the distinction between the so-called inner, greater jihad (*al-jihād al-akbar*) and outer, lesser jihad (*al-jihād al-aṣghar*), see Firestone 1999, 16–18.

4. It should be noted that this little book is simply a reprint of the chapter from

Smith's well-known *The World's Religions*, which is itself a lightly revised version of his 1958 book, *The Religions of Man*.

5.   This volume is a collection of essays first published in *Middle East Report*, a quarterly source of information on Middle East politics that has been in existence since 1971. Despite its so-called independence and its effort to address the "stereotypes and misconceptions" that, as phrased on the publication's website, plague Middle East coverage in the US press, the common distinction between authoritative "tradition" and distorted contemporary practice is evident in the editors' introduction. This should make clear that this rhetorical distinction is of use to virtually any political position (for more information see the *Report*'s website, http://www.merip.org/misc/about.html).

6.   Manji, a Toronto journalist and television personality who emigrated to Canada with her family from Uganda when she was four years old, refers to herself as a Muslim Refusenik, frankly noting on her opening page that she refuses to abide by "the self-appointed ambassadors of Islam" (2003, 1). Like Rushdie (whom she interviewed in 2002 and with whom she is pictured on her book's website), she calls for a reformation of the Islamic faith; like Cornell, improving the role of women, ensuring tolerance of religious minorities, addressing the problems that result from literalist readings of texts, and thereby recovering a lost tradition of free-thinking (*ijtihad*), are among her goals. As an openly lesbian woman, she also has great concern for improving the place of homosexuals in Muslim communities (p. 23). The website associated with the book can be found at www.muslim-refusenik.com.

7.   This quotation was transcribed from a recording of the speech that was available at   http://www.brothermalcolm.net/mxwords/whathesaid13.html.   The   recording was made on April 12, 1964, in Detroit, Michigan; the more familiar version of this speech, or at least the one that is cited as the basis for the print version found in many anthologies, was delivered a few days earlier, on April 3, at the Cory Methodist Church in Cleveland, OH, at a debate sponsored by the Congress of Racial Equality. For a text of that speech see George Breitman's edited volume, *Malcolm X Speaks* (1966, 23–44). My thanks to Ted Trost for bringing this speech to my attention; this speech is also cited in McCutcheon 2004b, 182.

8.   Of interest is the way in which those authors intent on celebrating religious diversity are able to distinguish between religious and political dissent and, in the process, lament the manner in which religious dissenters have too often been misunderstood by their peers (e.g., S. Stein 2003, x). That "the public expression of religious dissent" generally is limited either to pseudo-activity (ritual, domestic social practices, etc.) or violence that is exclusively projected inward at members of the group itself (e.g., the mass suicides at the People's Temple in Guyana in 1978 or Heaven's Gate in 1997), and not outward, should not go unnoticed. Should it be projected outward, it would more than likely be termed either an insurrection or a terrorist attack.

9.   See the interviews with bin Laden, available on the web: http://news.findlaw. com/cnn/docs/binLaden/binladenintvw-cnn.pdf (CNN's March 1997 interview); http://abcnews.go.com/sections/world/DailyNews/miller_binladen_980609.html (ABC News' May 1998 interview); and http://abcnews.go.com/sections/world/ DailyNews/transcript_binladen1_990110.html (ABC News' January 1999 interview). See Knox (2001) for a brief but sober analysis of these interviews; Knox, a reporter for the Toronto-based newspaper, *The Globe and Mail*, reads bin Laden not as an

enemy of freedom, as he has been portrayed from the start in much US commentary but—whether one agrees with bin Laden or not—as being in opposition to specific US foreign policies regarding the Middle East.

10. Even to compare their styles might strike some as blasphemous. For instance, see Ken Kurson's angry letter to the editor of the *Chicago Sun-Times* (March 15, 2003, Editorial Letters: 13) in which he notes that, because Lincoln stated on National Public Radio (in early March 2003) that "Bush and bin Laden are one and the same" (as Kurson phrased Lincoln's thesis), he is now ashamed to have attended the University of Chicago. That Lincoln had indeed compared both Bush's and bin Laden's rhetorical styles, and found significant similarities, rather than finding similarities in the truth of their words, was a point either willfully or inadvertently overlooked by Kurson in his rush to assert that the US's foreign policy "is on the right side of the battle for the world's soul." Lincoln made clear in a reply to Kurson published by the newspaper several days later (March 20, 2003, Editorial Letters: 34) that, contrary to Kurson's portrait, his analysis did not treat Bush and bin Laden as moral equivalents. "Rather," Lincoln writes, "I stress important differences between the two, while also identifying some less obvious commonalities in their rhetoric."

11. Before proceeding it is important to note Fish's work as the Dean of Liberal Arts and Sciences at the University of Illinois's campus at Chicago, and his attempts to press beyond the liberal consensus he so effectively critiques in his scholarship. For example, consider his hiring in 2000 of Paul Griffiths (formerly of the University of Chicago's Divinity School) into the Schmitt Chair of Catholic Studies. Griffiths, a recent convert to Roman Catholicism (as of 1996, as noted on his online CV), is well-known for his argument that religiously committed individuals bring a unique legitimacy to the study of religious commitment. That Fish seems not to have established, say, a Mormon Studies Chair, held by a Mormon, or a Jehovah's Witness Studies Chair, held by a member of the Jehovah's Witnesses, or, perhaps, an endowed Chair in Aryan Nation Studies held by…. I assume the reader gets the point; the predictably narrow range of his critique of liberalism ironically reinforces the very liberal, multiculturalism model he criticizes.

12. This observation is not so novel as it may seem, since the essentialist rhetorics that drive this constructive activity are shared with earlier generations of Orientalists.

13. Drake (2000, xvi) nicely makes this point with regard to many scholars' preoccupation with trying to assess whether or not Constantine's conversion to Christianity was sincere. If sincere, then it was a truly religious conversion, or so they argue; if it was not, then it was an instance of shallow political opportunism. Drake argues against efforts to recover the authentically religious beneath the crassly political that, in the case of scholarship on Constantine, he traces back to the Swiss historian, Jacob Burckhardt (1818–97), and his efforts to resuscitate the image of "the godly monarch who marches through Eusebius's pious pages" (2000, 12). Instead of sentimentalizing politics, Drake argues in favor of a thoroughly political analysis of the Constantinian rule, observing that "politics as a distinct field of inquiry is the study of a process; it has nothing to say about a given individual's religious sincerity or lack of same."

14. A transcript can be obtained at http://www.npr.org/features/feature.php?wfId=1403947.

15. The reference to saluting the flag is an allusion to Bush's September 17, 2001, speech in which he said that Muslim Americans love the US as much as he does, observing that they too salute the flag.

16. For more information, see the site Llewellyn established, http://courses.smsu. edu/jel807f/main3.html.

Chapter 6

1. As might be expected, Federal Democrats were not Pryor's only opponents; conservative Christian supporters of Judge Moore called for the President to drop his interest in appointing Pryor to the Federal Court. For instance, Rev. Frank Raddish, who is the founder and director of the Washington-based Capitol Hill Independent Baptist Ministries, held three rallies in Montgomery, the state capital, in the second half of 2003, in which President George W. Bush and state leaders were petitioned to: remove Pryor's name from consideration; to remove Judge Myron Thompson from the bench for his decision against Judge Moore; and to reinstate Judge Moore to the state Supreme Court.

2. See the *USA Today* newspaper column written by Pryor, at that time, in support of Moore (April 11, 1997: A14).

3. For background, see the August 23, 2003, CNN article on the case: http://www.cnn.com/2003/LAW/08/22/ten.commandments/.

4. The state's 1901 Constitution is posted at http://alisdb.legislature.state.al.us/acas/ACASLogin.asp.

5. Of interest is that the state of Kentucky ratified the 14th Amendment as late as March 18, 1976, after having rejected its ratification on January 8, 1867.

6. The first state to ratify the Amendment was Connecticut, on June 25, 1866, just twelve days after it was introduced in the US Congress.

7. This is somewhat reminiscent of David Hume's *The Natural History of Religion* (1757) in which he took for granted the existence of a Creator (as he writes in the Introduction: "The whole frame of nature bespeaks an intelligent author; and no rational enquirer can, after serious reflection, suspend his belief a moment with regard to the primary principles of genuine Theism and Religion" [1957, 21]), yet was puzzled over how human beings came to know about the existence of the Creator. Rejecting the notion of revealed religion, Hume opts instead for a notion of natural religion, whereby early humans inferred the existence of God from their observations of the natural world.

8. For the time being, it seems to have helped. On February 20, 2004, it was announced that President Bush would use his right to bypass temporarily the usual Congressional confirmation process by making a "recess appointment" to place Pryor in an empty seat on the 11th US Circuit Court of Appeals. The recess appointment, which has so far been used only twice by Bush, seems to have been placed in the US Constitution (see Article 2, Section 3, "The President shall have power to fill up all vacancies that may happen during the recess of the Senate, by granting commissions which shall expire at the end of their next session") to enable a president to ensure the government continues to function properly during a recess—though it has

developed into an all-purpose executive tool presidents use when frustrated in their appointments.

9. It should go without saying that identifying any one use of violence as a "first strike" is itself a judgement that deeply implicates the observer in reproducing but one side's grievances against the other. It would be more accurate to refer to all uses of violence as retaliation.

10. See *The New York Times* (October 15, 2003) in which it is reported that the Pentagon had decided no longer to allow the former three Islamic organizations upon which they relied to recommend Muslim chaplains to the military and the prison system. This issue seems to have arisen as a result of the unspecified charges (rumored to have been carrying "classified documents" out of the prison facility) the US military brought against one of its chaplains, Captain James "Youssef" Yee—a Chinese-American convert to Islam who served in Saudi Arabia during the first Gulf War—stationed at Guantanamo Bay, Cuba. Yee was certified as a Muslim chaplain by the Graduate School of Islamic and Social Sciences in Leesburg, VA—one of the three traditional certifying bodies for Muslim military chaplains which in 2002 came under investigation for possibly funding the al Qaeda organization. As reported in a September 23, 2003, press release from the office of Senator Charles Shummer (Democrat, New York, and member of the terrorism sub-committee): "In order to become a chaplain in the US Army, a prospective candidate must obtain an ecclesiastical endorsement from his faith group that certifies that person as a qualified member of a clergy group who is sensitive to religious pluralism and able to minister to people of all religions" (http://www.senate.gov/~schumer/SchumerWebsite/pressroom/press_releases/PR02043. html). In his press release, Shumer drew explicit attention to the set of criteria that ought to be used in adjudicating the authenticity of religious specialists sanctioned by the nation-state:

> In a letter to the Defense Department IG [Inspector General] this week, Schumer wrote … "It is disturbing that organizations with possible terrorist connections and *religious teachings contrary to American pluralistic values* hold the sole responsibility for Islamic instruction in our armed forces. It is certainly disappointing given that there are numerous American Muslim organizations with pristine reputations who are able to perform such activities." (emphasis added)

11. Said therefore concludes: "It is not the thesis of this book to suggest that there is such a thing as a real or true Orient (Islam, Arab, or whatever); nor is it to make an assertion about the necessary privilege of an 'insider' perspective over an 'outsider' one" (1979, 322).

12. Pascal wrote: "To obtain anything from God, the external must be joined to the internal. This means that we must kneel, pray with the lips, etc., in order that proud man, who would not submit to God, may now be subject to the creature. To expect help from these externals is superstition; to refuse to join them with the internal is to be proud" (1960, 197, fragment 722, following the numbering of M. Louis Lafuma).

13. Althusser's classic examples of interpellation are: the "Who's there?" question that follows the knock on the door, to which one answers, "It's me"; being hailed in the street, "Hello, my friend" to which one replies with a handshake or a nod of

the head; or a policeman yelling, "Hey, you there." In all cases a person recognizes him or herself as a certain type of subject given the manner in which they are addressed (e.g., as visitor, as friend, as criminal, etc.). Althusser therefore concludes that "ideology hails or interpellates individuals as subjects."

14. The chapters in this book draw upon and further work published in McCutcheon 2001, 2003, 2004a, 2004b, and 2004c. Moreover, whether the work of the following authors is cited or not, the preceding argument is indebted to the work of such writers as William Arnal (2000, 2001); Talal Asad (1993, 1999, 2003); Daniel Dubuisson (2003); Tim Fitzgerald (1997); Gary Lease (1994); Attila Molnár (2002); and Malory Nye (2000).

Bibliography

Adorno, Theodor. 1997 [1964]. *The Jargon of Authenticity*. Trans. Knut Tarnowski and Frederic Wills. Evanston, IL: Northwestern University Press.

—2002 [1991]. *The Culture Industry: Selected Essays on Mass Culture*. Ed. and intro. J. M. Bernstein. London and New York: Routledge.

Ali, Ahmed, trans. 1988 [1984]. *Al-Qur'ān: A Contemporary Translation*. Princeton, NJ: Princeton University Press.

Ali, Teriq. 2002. *The Clash of Fundamentalisms: Crusades, Jihads, and Modernity*. London: Verso.

Althusser, Louis. 1971. "Ideology and Ideological State Apparatuses (Notes Toward an Investigation." In Ben Brewster trans., *Lenin and Other Essays*, 127–86. New York and London: Monthly Review Press.

Anzaldua, Gloria. 1987. *Borderlands/La Frontera: The New Mestiza*. San Francisco: spinters/aunt lute.

Armstrong, Karen. 1993. *A History of God: The 4,000-Year Quest of Judaism, Christianity, and Islam*. New York: Ballantine Books.

—2000. *Islam: A Short History*. New York: The Modern Library.

—2001. "The True, Peaceful Face of Islam." *Time* (October 1): 48.

Arnal, William E. 2000). "Definition." In Willi Braun and Russell T. McCutcheon, eds., *Guide to the Study of Religion*, 21–34. London: Cassell.

—2001. "The Segregation of Social Desire: 'Religion' and Disney World." *Journal of the American Academy of Religion* 69: 1–19.

Arweck, Elisabeth, and Martin D. Stringer, eds. 1999. *Theorizing Faith: The Insider/Outsider Problem in the Study of Ritual*. Birmingham, UK: The University of Birmingham Press.

Asad, Talal. 1993. *Genealogies of Religion: Discipline and Reasons of Power in Christianity and Islam*. Baltimore: Johns Hopkins University Press.

—1999. "Religion, Nation-state, Secularism." In Peter van der Veer and Hartmut Lehmann, eds., *Nation and Religion: Perspectives on Europe and Asia*, 178–96. Princeton: Princeton University Press.

—2003. *Formations of the Secular: Christianity, Islam, Modernity*. Stanford, CA: Stanford University Press.

Ayoub, Mahmoud M. 1996. "The Islamic Tradition." In Willard G. Oxtoby, ed., *World Religions: Western Traditions*, 352–491. New York: Oxford University Press.

Beinin, Joel, and Joe Stork, eds. 1997. *Political Islam: Essays from Middle East Report*. Berkeley: University of California Press.

Berg, Herbert. 2000. *The Development of Exegesis in Early Islam: The Authenticity of Muslim Literature from the Formative Period*. Richmond, Surrey: Curzon.

Bishop, Ryan, and John Phillips 2002. "Manufacturing Emergencies." *Theory, Culture & Society* 19/4: 91–102.

Blanchère, Régis, trans. 1966. *Le Coran (al-Qor'ân)*. Paris: G.-P. Maisonneuve & Larose.

Bourdieu, Pierre. 1987. "What Makes a Social Class? On the Theoretical and Practical Existence of Groups." *Berkeley Journal of Sociology* 37: 1–17.

—1998 [1994]. *Practical Reason: On the Theory of Action*. Stanford: University of California Press.

Braun, Willi. 2000. "Religion." In Willi Braun and Russell T. McCutcheon, eds., *Guide to the Study of Religion*, 3–18. London: Cassell.

Breitman, George, ed. 1966. *Malcolm X Speaks: Selected Speeches and Statements*. New York: Grove.

Brown, Peter. 2003. *A Life of Learning*. American Council of Learned Societies Occasional Paper Series, no. 55. New York: ACLS.

Burgin, Victor. 1990 [1986]. *The End of Art Theory: Criticism and Postmodernity*. Atlantic Highlands, NJ: Humanities Press.

Chibnik, Michael. 2003. *Crafting Tradition: The Making of Oaxacan Wood Carvings*. Austin, TX: Universsity of Texas Press.

Chomsky, Noam. 2003. *Hegemony or Survival: America's Quest for Global Dominance*. New York: Metropolitan Books.

Colas, Dominique. 1997 [1992]. *Civil Society and Fanaticism: Conjoined Histories*. Trans. Amy Jacobs. Stanford: Stanford University Press.

Cornell, Vincent J. 2003. "A Muslim to Muslims: Reflections after September 11." In Stanley Hauerwas and Frank Lentricchia, eds., *Dissent from the Homeland: Essays After September 11*, 83–94. Durham, NC: Duke University Press.

Darnton, Robert 2003a. *George Washington's False Teeth: An Unconventional Guide to the Eighteenth Century*. New York: Norton.

—2003b. "The Heresies of Bibliography." *The New York Review of Books* 50/9 (May 29): 43–45.

Dawood, N. J., trans. 1983 [1956]. *The Koran*. London and New York: Penguin Books.

DeMott, Benjamin. 2003. "Junk Politics: A Voter's Guide to the Post-Literate Election." *Harper's Magazine* (November): 35–43.

Denny, Frederick M. 1987. *Islam and the Muslim Community*. San Franscisco: HarperSanFrancisco.

Didion, Joan. 2001 [1979]. *The White Album*. New York: Farrar, Straus, & Giroux.

Douglas, Mary. 1991 [1966]. *Purity and Danger: An Analysis of the Concepts of Pollution and Taboo*. London and New York: Routledge.

Drake, H. A. 2000. *Constantine and the Bishops: The Politics of Intolerance*. Baltimore, MD: Johns Hopkins University Press.

Dubuisson, Daniel. 2003 [1998]. *The Western Construction of Religion: Myths, Knowledge, and Ideology*. Trans. William Sayers. Baltimore and London: Johns Hopkins University Press.

Dunn, James D. G. 1990 [1977]. *Unity and Diversity in the New Testament: An Inquiry into the Character of Earliest Christianity*. 2nd ed. London: SCM; Philadelphia: Trinity Press International.

Erofeyev, Victor. 2002. "The Russian God." *The New Yorker* (December 16): 56–63.

Esposito, John L. 1999 [1992]. *The Islamic Threat: Myth or Reality*. 3rd ed. New York: Oxford University Press.

—2003. *Unholy War: Terror in the Name of Islam*. New York: Oxford University Press.

Esposito, John L., Darrell J. Fasching, and Todd Lewis. 2002. *World Religions Today*. New York: Oxford University Press.

Euben, Roxanne L. 1999. *Enemy in the Mirror: Islamic Fundamentalism and the Limits of Modern Rationalism*. Princeton: Princeton University Press.

Fakhry, Majid, trans. 2002 [2000]. *An Interpretation of the Qur'an. English Translation of the Meaning. A Bilingual Edition*. Washington Square, NY: New York University Press.

Farber, Daniel A., and Suzanna Sherry. 2002. *Desperately Seeking Certainty: The Misguided Quest for Constitutional Foundations*. Chicago: University of Chicago Press.

Fest, Joachim. 2001. *Speer: The Final Verdict*. Trans. Ewald Osers and Alexandra Dring. London: Weidenfeld & Nicolson.

Firestone, Reuven. 1999. *Jihād: The Origins of Holy War in Islam*. New York: Oxford University Press.

Fish, Stanley. 1999 [1995]. *Professional Correctness: Literary Studies and Political Change*. Cambridge, MA: Harvard University Press.

—2002. "Postmodern Warfare: The Ignorance of our Warrior Intellectuals." *Harper's Magazine* (July): 33–40.

Fitzgerald, Tim. 1997. "A Critique of the Concept of Religion." *Method & Theory in the Study of Religion* 9: 91–110.

Foucault, Michel. 1973. *This is Not a Pipe*. Trans. and ed. James Harkness. Berkeley, CA: University of California Press.

—1988. *Technologies of the Self: A Seminar with Michel Foucault*. Eds. Luther H. Martin, Huck Gutman, and Patrick H. Hutton. Amherst: University of Massachusetts Press.

—1989 [1969]. *The Archaeology of Knowledge*. Trans. A. M. Sheridan Smith. London and New York: Routledge.

Fowler, W. Warde. 1908. "The Latin History of the Word 'Religio'." In *Transactions of the Third International Congress for the History of Religions*, vol. 2, 169–75. Oxford: Clarendon Press.

—1933 [1909]. *Social Life at Rome in the Age of Cicero*. New York: Macmillan.

Fuller, Graham E. 2003. *The Future of Political Islam*. New York: Palgrave.

Geertz, Clifford. 1968. *Islam Observed: Religious Development in Morocco and Indonesia*. New Haven, CT: Yale University Press.

—2003a. "Which Way to Mecca?" *New York Review of Books* 50/10 (June 12): 27–30.

—2003b. "Which Way to Mecca? Part II." *New York Review of Books* 50/11 (July 3): 36–39.

Ghadbian, Najib. 1997. *Democratization and the Islamist Challenge in the Arab World*. Boulder, CO: Westview Press.

Glassé, Cyril. 1989. *The Concise Encyclopedia of Islam*. Intro. Huston Smith. San Francisco: Harper & Row.

Goldschmidt, Henry, and Elizabeth McAlister, eds. 2004. *Race, Nation, and Religion in the Americas*. New York: Oxford University Press.

Grainge, Paul. 1999. "Reclaiming Heritage: Colourization, Culture Wars and the Politics of Nostalgia." *Cultural Studies* 13/4: 621–38.

Griffiths, Paul J. 2000. "The Very Idea of Religion." *First Things* 103 (May): 30–35.

Hauerwas, Stanley. 1977. "Self-deception and Autobiography: Reflections on Speer's *Inside the Third Reich*." In Stanley Hauerwas, Richard Bondi, and David B. Burrell, eds., *Truthfulness and Tragedy: Further Investigations in Christian Ethics*, 82–98. Notre Dame: University of Notre Dame Press.

Horkheimer, Max, and Theodor W. Adorno. 2002 [1987]. "The Culture Industry: Enlightenment as Mass Deception." In Gunzelin Schmid Noerr, ed. and Edmund Jephcott, trans., *Dialectic of Enlightenment: Philosophical Fragments*, 94–136. Stanford, CA: Stanford University Press.

Hume, David. 1957 [1757]. *The Natural History of Religion*. Ed. H. E. Root. Stanford, CA: Stanford University Press.

Huntington, Samuel P. 1996. *The Clash of Civilizations and the Remaking of World Order*. New York: Simon & Schuster.

James, William. 1985 [1902]. *The Varieties of Religious Experience: A Study in Human Nature*. Ed. and intro. Martin E. Marty. New York and London: Penguin Books.

—2002 [1902]. *The Varieties of Religious Experience: A Study in Human Nature*. Centenary Edition. Foreword Micky James, intro. Eugene Taylor, and Jeremy Carrette. London and New York: Routledge.

Johnson, Paul C. 2002. "Death and Memory at Ground Zero: A Historian of Religion's Report." *Bulletin of the Council of Societies for the Study of Religion* 31/1: 3–7.

Johnson, Richard 2002. "Defending Ways of Life: The (Anti-)Terrorist Rhetorics of Bush and Blair." *Theory, Culture & Society* 19/4: 211–31.

Jurgensmeyer, Mark. 2001 [2000]. *Terror in the Mind of God: The Global Rise of Religious Violence*. Updated edition with a new preface. Berkeley, CA: University of California Press.

Kimball, Charles. 2002. *When Religion Becomes Evil*. San Francisco: HarperSan-Francisco.

Kirsch, Jonathan. 2001. *The Woman Who Laughed at God: The Untold History of the Jewish People*. New York: Viking.

Knox, Paul. 2001. "What Does He Want?" *The Globe and Mail* (19 September): A13.

Krugman, Paul R. 2004. "The Wars of the Texas Succession." *The New York Review of Books* 51/3 (February 26): 4–6.

Lawrence, Bruce. 1989. *Defenders of God: The Fundamentalist Revolt Against the Modern Age*. New York: Harper & Row.

Lease, Gary. 1994. "The History of 'Religious' Consciousness and the Diffusion of Culture: Strategies for Surviving Dissolution." *Historical Reflections/Reflexions Historiques* 20: 453–79.

LeMaire, André. 2002. "Burial Box of James the Brother of Jesus: Earliest Archaeological Evidence of Jesus Found in Jerusalem." *Biblical Archaeology Review* 28/6 (November/December): 24–33, 70.

Lewis, Bernard. 2003 [2002]. *What Went Wrong? The Clash Between Islam and Modernity in the Middle East*. New York: Perennial.

—(2004) [2003]. *The Crisis of Islam: Holy War and Unholy Terror*. New York: Random House.

Lewis, B. Ch. Pellat, and J. Schacht, eds. 1965. *The Encyclopaedia of Islam*. New edition. Vol. 2, C-G. Leiden: E. J. Brill.

Lightstone, Jack N. 1984. *The Commerce of the Sacred: Mediation of the Divine among Jews in the Graeco-Roman Diaspora*. Brown Judaic Studies, 59. Chico, CA: Scholars Press.

Lincoln, Bruce. 1989. *Discourse and the Construction of Society: Comparative Studies of Myth, Ritual, and Classification*. New York: Oxford University Press.

—1994. *Authority: Construction and Corrosion*. Chicago: University of Chicago Press.

—1996. "Theses on Method." *Method & Theory in the Study of Religion* 8/3: 225–27.

—2003. *Holy Terrors: Thinking about Religion after September 11*. Chicago: University of Chicago Press.

Lippman, Thomas W. 1995 [1982]. *Understanding Islam: An Introduction to the Muslim World*. New York: Meridian.

Lobdell, William, and Richard Winton. 2003. "Mahony Resisting Disclosure." *Los Angeles Times* (March 3, 2003): B1, B6.

Lopez, Donald S. Jr. 1998. *Prisoners of Shangri-La: Tibetan Buddhism and the West*. Chicago: University of Chicago Press.

MacFarquhar, Larissa. 2003a. "The Devil's Accountant." *The New Yorker* (March 31): 64–79.

—2003b. "The Movie Lover." *The New Yorker* (October 20): 146–59.

—2004. "The Populist." *The New Yorker* (February 16 and 23): 132–45.

Manji, Irshad. 2003. *The Trouble with Islam: A Muslim's Call for Reform in Her Faith*. New York: St. Martin's Press.

Marty, Martin. 1995. "Competing for God's Ear." *Christian Century* (April 19): 439.

—1997. *The One and the Many: America's Struggle for the Common Good*. Cambridge, MA: Harvard University Press.

Marx, Karl. 1977 [1844]. "Towards a Critique of Hegel's *Philosophy of Right*: Introduction." In David McLellan, ed., *Karl Marx: Selected Writings*, 63–74. New York: Oxford University Press.

Masuzawa, Tomoko. 1993. *In Search of Dreamtime: The Quest for the Origin of Religion*. Chicago: University of Chicago Press.

—2000a. "From Theology to World Religions: Ernst Troeltsch and the Making of *Religionsgeschichte*." In Tim Jensen and Mikael Rothstein, eds., *Secular Theories on Religion*, 149–66. Copenhagen: Museum Tusculanum Press.

—2000b. "Origin." In Willi Braun and Russell T. McCutcheon, eds., *Guide to the Study of Religion*, 209–24. London and New York: Continuum.

—(forthcoming a). *The Invention of World Religions, or How the Idea of European Hegemony Came to be Expressed in the Language of Pluralism and Diversity*. Chicago: University of Chicago Press.

—(forthcoming b). "World Religions." In Lindsay Jones, ed., *Encyclopedia of Religion*. 2nd ed. New York: Macmillan.

McCutcheon, Russell T. 1997. *Manufacturing Religion: The Discourse on Sui Generis Religion and the Politics of Nostalgia*. New York: Oxford University Press.

—ed. 1999. *The Insider/Outsider Problem in the Study of Religion: A Reader*. London and New York: Continuum.

—2001. *Critics Not Caretakers: Redescribing the Public Study of Religion*. Albany, NY: State University of New York Press.

—2003. *The Discipline of Religion: Structure, Meaning, Rhetoric*. London and New York: Routledge.

—2004a. "The Ideology of Closure and the Problem of the Insider/Outsider Problem in the Study of Religion." *Studies in Religion/Sciences Religieuses* 32/3: 337–52.

—2004b. "Religion, Ire, and Dangerous Things." *Journal of the American Academy of Religion* 72/1: 173–93.

—2004c. "'Religion' and the Problem of the Governable Self, or, How to Live in a Less than Perfect Nation." *Method & Theory in the Study of Religion* (forthcoming).

Molnár, Attila K. 2002. "The Construction of the Notion of Religion in Early Modern Europe." *Method & Theory in the Study of Religion* 14: 47–60.

Mori, Masahiro. 1999 [1974]. *The Buddha in the Robot: A Robot Engineer's Thoughts on Science and Religion*. Trans. Charles S. Terry. Tokyo: Kosei Publishing Co.

Mushembled, Robert. 2004. *A History of the Devil: From the Middle Ages to the Present*. Trans. Jean Birrell. Cambridge, UK: Polity Press.

Musil, Robert. 1996 [1952]. *The Man Without Qualities*, vol. 1. Trans. Sophie Wilkins. New York: Vintage International.

Naasr, Seyyed Hossein. 2002. *The Heart of Islam: Enduring Values for Humanity*. San Francisco: HarperSanFrancisco.

Nemtsov, A. V. 2002. "Alcohol-related Human Losses in Russia in the 1980s and 1990s." *Addiction* 97/11: 1413–25.

Nietzsche, Friedrich. 1986 [1878]. *Human All Too Human: A Book for Free Spirits*. Trans. R. J. Hollingdale. Cambridge: Cambridge University Press.

Nye, Malory. 2000. "Religion, Post-religionism, and Religioning: Religious Studies and Contemporary Cultural Debates." *Method & Theory in the Study of Religion* 12: 447–76.

Pascal, Blaise. 1960 [1670]. *Pensée: Notes on Religion and Other Subjects*. Ed. and intro. Louis Lafuma, trans. John Warrington. London: J. M. Dent & Sons.

Pinto, Maria do Céu. 1999. *Political Islam and the United States: A Study of US Policy towards Islamist Movements in the Middle East*. Reading, UK: Ithaca Press.

Powers, Thomas. 2003. "The Vanishing Case for War." *The New York Review of Books* 50/19 (December 4): 2–17.

Qutb, Sayyid. 1993 [1964]. *Milestones*. [*Ma'alim fil-Tariq*]. Foreword Ahmad Zaki Hammad. Indianapolis: American Trust Publications.

Rahmani, L. Y. 1994. *A Catalogue of Jewish Ossuaries in the Collection of the State of Israel*. Jerusalem: Israel Academy of Sciences and Humanities.

Reichardt, Jasia. 1978. *Robots: Fact, Fiction, and Prediction*. Harmondsworth and New York: Penguin Books.

Renard, John. 1996. *Seven Doors to Islam: Spirituality and the Religious Life of Muslims*. Berkeley, CA: University of California Press.

Roy, Oliver. 1994. *The Failure of Political Islam*. Trans. Carol Volk. Cambridge, MA: Harvard University Press.

Rushdie, Salman. 2001. "Yes, this is About Islam: How Radical Politics Co-opts a Faith." *The New York Times* (November 2): A25, cols. 1–4.

Ruthven, Malise. 1997. *Islam: A Very Short Introduction*. New York: Oxford University Press.

Said, Edward. 1979 [1978]. *Orientalism*. New York: Vintage.

—1997 [1981]. *Covering Islam: How the Media and the Experts Determine How We See the Rest of the World*. Revised ed. New York: Vintage.

—2002. "Impossible Histories: Why the Many Islams Cannot be Simplified." *Harper's Magazine* (July): 69–74.

Sanchez, Stephen H. 2002. "James Was Not a Midget!: Observations on a Visit to the James Ossuary Exhibit at the Royal Ontario Museum." http://www.bible. org/docs/soapbox/jamesossuary.htm.

Schlesinger, Arthur Jr. 2003. "Eyeless in Iraq." *The New York Review of Books* 50/16 (October): 24–27.

Schwartz, Stephen. 2002. *The Two Faces of Islam: The House of Sa'ud from Tradition to Terror*. New York: Doubleday.

Sedaris, David. 2003. "Tricked." *The New Yorker* (November 3): 50–53.

Sells, Michael, trans. and intro. 1999. *Approaching the Qur'an: The Early Revelations*. Ashland, OR: White Cloud.

Sereny, Gitta. 1995. *Albert Speer: His Battle With Truth*. Ed. Peter Dimock. New York: Vintage Books.

Shahrani, M. Nazif. 1991. "Local Knowledge of Islam and Social Discourse in Afghanistan and Turkistan in the Modern Period." In Robert L. Canfield, ed., *Turko-Persia in Historical Perspective*, 161–88. New York: Cambridge University Press.

Shanks, Hershel. 2003a. "Cracks in James Bone Box Repaired: Crowds Flock to Toronto Exhibit." *Biblical Archaeology Review* 29/1 (January/February): 20–25.

—2003b. "The 2002 Annual Meeting: Horsing Around in Toronto." *Biblical Archaeology Review* 29/2 (March/April): 50–59.

Shanks, Hershel, and Ben Witherington. 2003. *The Brother of Jesus: The Dramatic Story and Meaning of the First Archaeological Link to Jesus and his Family*. San Francisco: HarperSanFrancisco.

Shapiro, Faydra. 2003. "Autobiography and Ethnography: Falling in Love with the Inner Other." *Method & Theory in the Study of Religion* 15: 187–202.

Shnayerson, Michael. 2003. "Judging Andy." *Vanity Fair* (November): 196–219.

Smith, Huston. 2001. *Islam: A Concise Introduction*. San Francisco: HarperSanFrancisco.

Smith, Jonathan Z. 1982. *Imagining Religion: From Babylon to Jonestown*. Chicago: University of Chicago Press.

—1987. *To Take Place: Toward Theory in Ritual*. Chicago: University of Chicago Press.

—1990. *Drudgery Divine: On the Comparison of Early Christianities and the Religions of Late Antiquity*. Chicago: University of Chicago Press.

—1998. "Religion, Religions, Religious." In Mark C. Taylor, ed., *Critical Terms for Religious Studies*, 269–84. Chicago: University of Chicago Press.

Smith, Wilfred Cantwell. 1972 [1962]. *The Faith of Other Men*. New York: Harper Torchbooks.

—1991 [1962]. *The Meaning and End of Religion*. Foreword John Hick. Minneapolis, MN: Fortress Press.

Sontag, Susan. 2003. *Regarding the Pain of Others*. New York: Picador.

Speer, Albert. 1970 [1969]. *Inside the Third Reich: Memoirs*. Trans. Richard and Clara Winston, intro. Eugene Davidson. New York: Macmillan.

—1976. *Spandau: The Secret Diaries*. Trans. Richard and Clara Winston. New York: Macmillan.

Stein, Stephen J. 2003 [2000]. *Communities of Dissent: A History of Alternative Religions in America*. New York: Oxford University Press.

Stern, Jessica. 2003. *Terror in the Name of God: Why Religious Militants Kill*. New York: HarperCollins.

Strenski, Ivan. 2002. "Review of R. McCutcheon, *Critics Not Caretakers*." *Journal of the American Academy of Religion* 70/2: 427–30.

Sunstein, Cass R. 2003. *Why Societies Need Dissent*. Cambridge, MA: Harvard University Press.

Taylor, Charles. 1989. *Sources of the Self: The Making of the Modern Identity*. Cambridge, MA: Harvard University Press.

—1991. *The Ethics of Authenticity*. Cambridge, MA: Harvard University Press.

—2002. *Varieties of Religion Today: William James Revisited*. Cambridge, MA: Harvard University Press.

Thompson, E. P. 1980 [1963]. *The Making of the English Working Class*. London and New York: Penguin Books.

Toomey, Wilt Henry. 1954. *Religio: A Semantic Study of the Pre-Christian Use of the Terms Religio and Religiosus*. PhD dissertation, Columbia University. Ann Arbor, MI: UMI Dissertation Services.

Turner, Bryan S. 2002. "Sovereignty and Emergency: Political Theology, Islam, and American Conservatism." *Theory, Culture & Society* 19/4: 103–19.

Vowell, Sarah. 2002. *The Partly Cloudy Patriot*. New York: Simon & Schuster.

Waardenburg, Jacques. 2003. *Muslims and Others: Relations in Context*. Berlin and New York: Walter de Gruyter.

Wallerstein, Immanuel. 2000. "The Agonies of Liberalism." In *The Essential Wallerstein*, 416–34. New York: The New Press.

Wheen, Francis. 2001 [1999]). *Karl Marx: A Life*. New York: W. W. Norton.

Wittgenstein, Ludwig. 1968 [1953]. *Philosophical Investigations*. 3rd ed. Trans. G. E. N. Anscombe. New York: Macmillan.

Yavuz, M. Hakan. 2003. *Islamic Political Identity in Turkey*. New York: Oxford University Press.

Zant, Dan van der. 1997. *The Good Nazi: The Life and Lies of Albert Speer*. Boston: Houghton Mifflin.

Zinn, Howard. 2003 [1980]. *A People's History of the United States: 1492–Present*. New York: HarperCollins.

Žižek, Slavoj. 1997 [1994]. "Introduction: The Spectre of Ideology." In Slavoj Žižek, ed., *Mapping Ideology*, 1–33. London: Verso.

—2001. "The Matrix, or the Two Sides of Perversion." In *Enjoy Your Symptom: Jacques Lacan in Hollywood and Out*, 213–33. 2nd ed. New York: Routledge.

—2002. *Welcome to the Desert of the Real: Five Essays on September 11 and Related Dates*. London: Verso.

—2003. *The Puppet and the Dwarf: The Perverse Core of Christianity*. Cambridge, MA: MIT Press.

Index

DATE DUE
